RON JULIAN

RIGHTEOUS SINNERS

THE BELIEVER'S STRUGGLE WITH FAITH, GRACE, AND WORKS

"Biblically exact and pastorally profound, this book is a gem!"
–J.I. Packer

NAVPRESS
BRINGING TRUTH TO LIFE
NavPress Publishing Group
P.O. Box 35001, Colorado Springs, Colorado 80935

The Navigators is an international Christian organization. Our mission is to reach, disciple, and equip people to know Christ and to make Him known through successive generations. We envision multitudes of diverse people in the United States and every other nation who have a passionate love for Christ, live a lifestyle of sharing Christ's love, and multiply spiritual laborers among those without Christ.

NavPress is the publishing ministry of The Navigators. NavPress publications help believers learn biblical truth and apply what they learn to their lives and ministries. Our mission is to stimulate spiritual formation among our readers.

Library of Congress Catalog Card Number: 97-50490
ISBN 1-57683-057-8

Some of the anecdotal illustrations in this book are true to life and are included with the permission of the persons involved. All other illustrations are composites of real situations, and any resemblance to people living or dead is coincidental.

Unless otherwise identified, all Scripture quotations in this publication are taken from the *New American Standard Bible* (NASB), © The Lockman Foundation 1960, 1962, 1963, 1968, 1971, 1972, 1973, 1975, 1977. Words in italics have been emphasized by the author.

Julien, Ron, 1953-
    Righteous sinners : the believer's struggle with faith, grace, and works / Ron Julian.
        p.   cm.
    ISBN 1-57683-057-8 (pbk.)
    1. Salvation. 2. Grace (Theology). 3. Jesus Christ—Lordship. 4. Predestination. 5. Faith. 6. Law and gospel. I. Title.
BT751.2.J85   1998
234—dc21   97-50490
                                      CIP

Printed in the United States of America

1 2 3 4 5 6 7 8 9 10 11 12 13 14 15 / 02 01 00 99 98

FOR A FREE CATALOG OF
NAVPRESS BOOKS & BIBLE STUDIES,
CALL 1-800-366-7788 (USA)
OR 1-416-499-4615 (CANADA)

Contents

To Robby

Acknowledgments

⟨———

This book was written as part of my work at McKenzie Study Center in Eugene, Oregon. For sixteen years, the Study Center has provided an environment where I could study, teach, and discuss important issues with gifted people. It is a wonderful opportunity. Staff members Tony Arlyn, Larry Barber, Dick Booster, David Crabtree, Jack Crabtree, Wes Hurd, Kim Kimberling, Nancy Scott, and Margaret Sholaas have been very helpful and encouraging in the sometimes difficult writing process.

I owe many thanks to those who by their faithful support have given me the opportunity to work at McKenzie Study Center. I also want to thank the people, in addition to the Study Center staff, who read a preliminary version of the book and gave me helpful feedback: Bob Blanchard, Roger Ruddle, Denise Steele, and Terry and Deanna Stollar. Thanks also to my sister, Annette Reid, for her help and encouragement. And many thanks to my children, Brian and Erin, for their patience while their father experienced the trials of authorship. We're going to take that trip to the beach real soon.

I must thank two people in particular: (1) Jack Crabtree is a great Bible student and a great man. No other person has contributed more to my thinking on the Bible. (2) Robby Julian is my wife and God's great gift to me. She is a talented editor and has helped me with all phases of this book. It would not have happened without her.

Among the many pursuits of the McKenzie Study Center, one will always find a commitment to the inerrancy of the Bible, the sovereign grace of God, and the importance of principled exegesis. These commitments have also, I hope, informed the writing of this book.

All biblical quotations are from the New American Standard Bible, with the exception of certain changes in translation I have made. These are marked with an '*'.

In Search of True Christian Faith

This book was born twenty-five years ago on a very bad night. As a young Christian (I converted at nineteen) I struggled greatly with the sin that was all too noticeable in my life. Some of my teachers at the time believed in the "victorious Christian life" theology. Victory over sin was mine, they taught, if I would just walk by the Spirit, if I would just "let go and let God." I tried, with all the faith I could muster, to do just that. It didn't seem to work. However I tried to "let go," I found myself just as much a prisoner of selfishness and lust as I was before. One night— the bad night—I confessed this frankly to one of our leaders and asked for help. His answer changed my life.

He told me that since "walking by the Spirit" wasn't working for me, it probably meant I wasn't a Christian at all. There was no hope for me unless this time I "really" believed God. After hearing this, I went for a long walk into the night, troubled and confused. Could he be right? I didn't know how to believe any harder than I already had. I remember standing under a street lamp and crying out inside, "No, he's not right! I am a believer; I do want what God has promised in the gospel!" Stung by this well-meant but disturbing counsel, I began the first serious theological reflections of my life. If there was nothing "wrong" with my faith and yet I still struggled with sin, then maybe that struggle was a natural part of the Christian life. Maybe I had enough faith already; maybe I could count on God to purge the crud from my soul in His own good time. I thought of the verse in Philippians: "He who began a good work in you will perfect it until the day of Christ Jesus." I didn't understand this verse entirely, but what I did understand comforted me. God

Himself was doing His work in me. My faith was the beginning of that work; my moral perfection would be its completion. I could take heart: God was at work from beginning to end, saving even sinners like me.

On that night two things happened. Most important, this was one of a number of times when God graciously reached out to me, to teach me to love and to trust Him more. But I also realized something else that night: On the most important questions of our faith, Christians do not always agree. That night began the great quest of my life to understand the Bible for myself, especially those parts which dealt with the nature of saving faith. In a sense, that night I started writing this book.

I tell this story because no author is without biases, and it is just as well you know mine. The theological questions we'll explore together are not academic to me; they are the fundamental questions of my life, and I have a great deal at stake in the answers. Have I succeeded in being objective? I want to be. I can say the Bible has surprised me; that guy standing under the lamppost would have been puzzled by what I believe today. You must evaluate my arguments, not my passion; but it is best that you know the passion is there. All of the "academic" work I have done in the Bible in the past twenty-five years has been motivated by one thing: A desire to understand the gospel and its implications.

The most recent and specific motivation for my writing comes from the recurring debate over lordship salvation. That debate addresses the theological questions I find most striking: What does saving faith look like? How can I know I am a true believer? How should I understand the problem of sin in my own life? Although I set out to respond point for point to recent books on this topic, I have decided to chart my own course; only incidentally will I address specific arguments made by one side or the other in that debate. I hope and believe that the position I take avoids problems found on both sides of the debate.

This book is for those who believe, as I do, that theology is a matter of life and death. How many of us still exist, I don't know. I do know that theology, when it is not ignored altogether, is often scorned as "divisive"; theological questions are ridiculed as "head knowledge, not heart knowledge." Such criticisms are not totally unjust. Theology can be used in evil ways: as a weapon; as an intellectual game; even as a shield behind which we hope to hide from God. However, just because a tool can be misused doesn't mean we toss it out. A hammer can be used to kill; shall we drive nails with our bare hands? Theology is a tool, and we *must not* throw it away; we *cannot* throw it away. We are all theologians, either good ones or bad ones. Life is a journey, either toward the truth or away from it, and all of the most important truths are theological.

Am I suggesting our salvation is dependent on the accuracy of our theology? Well, yes and no. The Bible connects our salvation with what we believe; it also connects our salvation with what we do. How the Bible connects our salvation, our beliefs, and our actions is the topic we are about to explore. For now, all I am saying is this: Doing theology is our life's work.

Not everyone is called to write books of theology (for which we should be grateful!), but we all must ask and answer inescapable questions about our own existence. We can pretend such questions are irrelevant, but that only means we have already answered the questions wrongly. According to the Bible, if we are not given over to pursuing the knowledge of God and the knowledge of ourselves in relationship to God, then we are pursuing the wrong things.

This book is intended to help anyone who is wrestling with the biggest theological question of all: What does it mean to be a person of faith? If you have never struggled with your own moral weaknesses, if you have never looked in the mirror and wondered whether a believer was staring back at you, if you have never felt a twinge of terror while reading "Not everyone who says to me 'Lord, Lord,' will enter into the kingdom of heaven," then this discussion may not interest you. For me, the issues I address are the central questions of my life. I became a student of the Bible because I wanted to know what genuine Christian faith looks like. If this is your desire as well, then I invite you to join me in the search.

PART ONE

THE TENSION AT THE HEART OF THE GOSPEL

CHAPTER ONE

The Dilemma of Grace

—

Over many years as a believer, Joe has felt an increasing tension in his life as a Christian. He can't quite fit together the pieces of his life with the pieces of his theology. Certainly he finds his experience ambiguous. The promises of God are becoming increasingly precious to him, and he can honestly say he loves God more than he ever has. But his own actions and attitudes puzzle and disturb him. Sin seems to have him in as strong a grip as ever. He thinks wistfully of his younger days, when obedience seemed simple and easy to do. But these days he is a husband, father, breadwinner, and church elder; these days temptations come at him faster than he can even begin to cope with. He tries, but he can't seem to stop being impatient with his children, testy with his wife, fearful at work, and weary of the demanding, crabby people at church. He has long since despaired of taming his sexual attitudes; he will never be unfaithful to his wife, but he would be ashamed for her to know what goes on in his head. Joe can't help asking himself certain questions: *Is this how a believer, a follower of Christ, and lover of God is supposed to be? Can I make a credible claim to be a Christian when my heart is still filled with such selfishness and lust?*

For some time now Joe has had a growing desire to dig into the Bible and see what it says about his situation. But so far, he finds a similar ambiguity he can't resolve. The apostle Paul says we are saved by faith apart from works (Romans 3:28), but James says we are justified by works and not by faith alone (James 2:24). Jesus tells us the only "work" God requires is to believe in Him (John 6:29), but then says if we don't forgive others we won't be forgiven ourselves (Matthew 6:15). Jesus says invitingly, "The one who comes to Me I will certainly not cast out" (John 6:37), but also says, "Depart from Me, you who practice lawlessness" (Matthew 7:23). Caught between the seeming ambiguities in his Bible and in his life, Joe is left with some crucial questions: *How can I know I am saved? Am I supposed to have conquered sin in my life? What if I can't? What is God asking of me, anyway?*

Recently Joe has become familiar with the "lordship salvation" debate. One side in that debate (in this book I call them "free salvationists") argues that salvation comes through a simple acceptance of Jesus as *Savior*. Salvation is not *dependent* on obedience and righteous living, as worthy as those things are. Joe finds this thought attractive and comforting. However, he keeps running into things in the Bible that seem to contradict it. He can't dismiss the arguments of the "lordship salvationists" who argue that salvation only comes to those who accept Jesus as *Lord*, which means submitting to His rule, repenting of sin, and living an obedient life. Joe sees much in the Bible that seems to say that very thing. However, this does not comfort Joe; instead it comes close to terrifying him. How could anyone who fails as often as Joe does claim to be "obedient"? The debate over lordship salvation has left Joe with more uncertainties than he had before.

THE DILEMMA

It sounds strange to say, but the grace of God seems to present us with a dilemma. On the one hand, grace frees us from obligation. Grace says, "I will bless you even though you don't deserve it." On the other hand, no one receives grace who has not met certain obligations. Sinners can find grace, but not sinners who refuse to believe God's promises, or who hate God, or who reject Jesus. In one sense, grace is a suspension of requirements—even though we don't qualify, God saves us. Yet in another sense, grace only comes to those who meet certain requirements—if we don't qualify, God will not save us. Rebels like ourselves can find pardon, but only if (in some sense) we are no longer rebels. Any bum can come to this banquet, but he must be wearing his wedding clothes. Thus our dilemma: If we try to talk about the requirements for salvation, we are in danger of ignoring grace; if we try to emphasize grace, we are in danger of ignoring the very real requirements for salvation.

Obviously, resolving this dilemma is very important, but how shall we do that? The Reformation claimed to have found the answer: We are not required to be without "sin," but we are required to have "faith." But that only resolves the dilemma if we can agree on what "sin" and "faith" *mean.* This is far from an academic question. In the history of the church, vastly different gospels have been preached, each determined by an understanding of words like "sin," "faith," "justification," "works," and so on. Furthermore, such questions reach into the heart of the Christian life, as our friend Joe could tell us. Does sin call our salvation into question? Does obedience prove we are saved?

Take any serious sin as an example. Could a man commit adultery and still claim to be saved? If I were to say, "No, he couldn't," a myriad of Christians would rise up and call me a "legalist." That is, they would charge I am *connecting* salvation with obedience to the moral law. If I were to say, "Yes, he could," a myriad of Christians would rise up and call me an "antinomian" (from *nomos,* "law"). That is, they would charge me with *disconnecting* salvation from obedience to the moral law. "Legalist" and "antinomian" are two of our worst theological swear words; no one wants to be called either one.

But are we doomed to be one or the other? If we rebel at the self-righteousness and pride associated with legalism, must we become antinomians? If we rebel at the self-indulgence associated with the antinomian, must we become legalists? Martin

Luther compared us to drunks who, in trying to avoid falling off one side of the horse, end up falling off the other. But is there even a horse in the middle to sit on?

Now consider obedience. Imagine a man has turned from his former adulterous ways. His friends still sleep around with great abandon, but he has changed. He has vowed to remain faithful to his wife, and in fact he succeeds at this. He sees this as real progress, and he regularly prays to thank God for his deliverance. On the one hand, this sounds very right. Paul says "we are His workmanship, created in Christ Jesus for good works, which God prepared beforehand, that we should walk in them" (Ephesians 2:10). What could be more fitting than to thank God for delivering us from sin? On the other hand, Jesus tells a story about a Pharisee who prays, "God, I thank Thee that I am not like other people: swindlers, unjust, adulterers . . . " (Luke 18:11). The Pharisee is thanking God for making him a moral man, but God sees this prayer as an abomination; Jesus tells us God rejects the Pharisee altogether. It seems as if traps await on every side — traps if we presume to see goodness in our lives; traps if we presume to be saved without goodness.

If grace were not grace, then there would be no dilemma. All of us would get what we deserve, and this would be very easy to understand. Goodness would be rewarded, evil would be punished, and our works would mean everything. Equally, the doctrine of "universalism" would eliminate the dilemma. If God saved all of us, then none of us would get what we deserve, and this too would be very easy to understand. Our works would mean nothing. But neither of these simple extremes is true. It all comes back to Paul and James again: We are not justified by works, and yet we are. In one sense what we are is irrelevant to our salvation; in another sense what we are determines our salvation. If the Bible is true and coherent (and I believe it is), then we can't ignore either idea. Both truths must be maintained, and both must be reconciled. This is the central tension in Christian theology and in Christian living.

THE DEBATE

Before he began struggling to resolve this tension, our friend Joe took it for granted that all Christians embrace the same gospel: a message of grace, offering salvation to all who have faith, in spite of our works. Joe has found, however, that it's not so simple. The lordship salvation debate asks the question, "Can we accept Jesus merely as Savior, or must we also accept Him as Lord?" However, the essence of this debate cannot be captured in a single slogan. Each side disagrees with the other on a whole series of issues. To illustrate this, let us consider how two fictional counselors would answer Joe's pressing questions about his own salvation. (I emphasize "fictional." Although these answers represent my understanding of real arguments being made today, I am not claiming to speak for anyone else.)

A Free Salvationist Counsels Joe

What must I do to be saved? Joe, have you ever sincerely believed that Jesus is the Christ whom God raised from the dead? If you have, then you are saved. Salvation comes to anyone who has "faith," and faith is nothing more than believing the correct doctrines about Jesus. Such faith is simple to accomplish and easy to identify. That is why "salvation by faith" is so gracious. You need do nothing except change your mind about Jesus.

Is my salvation secure? If so, how? Once you believe, Joe, your salvation is secure, because saving faith is a one-time event, an irrevocable act that secures salvation no matter what you go on to do. In this way God makes your salvation secure and yet allows you free will. If later you should stop believing, that is your free choice. However, this will not stop God from saving you. Salvation is a one-way street, a switch you can only turn "on" but not "off" again. God ensures the salvation of one-time believers by ignoring any subsequent free-will decision they might make.

Can I know I am saved? If so, how? How could you *not* know you are saved, Joe? Doesn't the Bible promise salvation to all who believe? Well, do you believe? If you do, that settles it.

To believe that Jesus is the risen Christ is a simple matter; surely you could not be mistaken about your own beliefs. Further self-examination is irrelevant since there is no necessary connection between saving faith and an obedient life.

In what sense is my salvation "not by works"? You believe that Jesus is the risen Christ, Joe, and that is all God requires for salvation. Anything else—anything—is by definition a "work." Such works are unnecessary for salvation. Repentance? Repentance is good, but it is a work and unnecessary for salvation. Obedience? Obedience is good, but it is a work and unnecessary for salvation. Loving God? Fearing God? Confessing sin? Abandoning worldliness? Forgiving your brother? Such things are all very good, but they are all works and unnecessary for salvation.

Now I know the Bible has countless passages that seem to connect our salvation with the way we live. How can "repentance," "obedience," and so on be irrelevant to salvation when the Bible seems to insist they are essential? That's the key, Joe; they only *seem* to connect salvation and works. These passages can be explained if we remember two common errors in interpretation.

1. In some passages, we mistakenly assume salvation is the issue when in fact it is not. Many problem passages can be solved if we remember salvation *is not* the issue; present blessings or future rewards are at stake, not salvation. The Bible tells us that when we repent and obey, our lives will be blessed in this present world. It also promises us rewards at Christ's judgment seat. Our works determine the level of blessing we receive from God but have nothing to do with our salvation.

2. In other passages, salvation is indeed the issue, but we misunderstand what the commands to "obey," to "repent," and so on really mean. We "repent" and we "obey" by changing our doctrinal beliefs about Jesus. Although these passages sound like they are describing works, closer examination shows they are just describing doctrinal belief in a different way.

So in fact, Joe, the Bible *never* connects works and salvation, even though it might look as if it does.

A Lordship Salvationist Counsels Joe

Joe gets a very different set of answers from a hypothetical counselor on the other side in this debate.

What must I do to be saved? Salvation comes to the one who has faith, but faith involves much more than mere doctrinal beliefs. Faith is an active trust in God, a dynamic commitment of the heart and will. True believers totally surrender to God, yielding their lives to Him in obedience. Thus the mere fact that you believe the correct doctrines about Jesus is no indication you are saved. Many who are not true children of God can nevertheless honestly say they believe that Jesus is the risen Christ. True faith must be lived out, and it inevitably leads to good works.

Is my salvation secure? If so, how? Yes, Joe, if you have totally surrendered to God and are a true believer, you cannot lose your salvation. This is not to say, however, that your future choices do not matter; they matter very much indeed. You must persevere in faith and obedience for your entire life. God does not ignore your later choices; He works through those choices, ensuring that you continue to follow Him. If you are a true child of God, your salvation is secure because God will preserve your belief and commitment to Him throughout your life.

Can I know I am saved? If so, how? Since mere assent to the doctrines about Christ does not prove we are saved, you may be wondering what does. Because faith is complex, dynamic, and life-changing, genuine faith is shown by its effect on your life. Repentance, obedience, good works, and so on are the inevitable result of a genuine faith. Your perseverance and growth in godliness mark you as a true child of God. So you can see, Joe, that self-examination is essential to assurance of salvation. True believers will have a certain look in this life, so you will need to examine your own life to see if you fit the description.

In what sense is my salvation "not by works"? Joe, you are not earning your salvation through your works; you can make no claim before God that you deserve His blessing because of your good works. Good works are the *fruit* of being forgiven by God, not the *cause*. Still, such fruit is inevitable. Without such fruit, any claim to be saved must be suspect. The true child of God is the one who repents, obeys, fears God, loves God, confesses sin, abandons worldliness, forgives others, and much more.

Now I know countless passages in the Bible seem to deny that salvation has anything to do with our works. And that's the key: Those passages only *seem* to disconnect salvation and works. It will help if you will remember the following truths:

1. We are not being saved because we have good works; better to say we have good works because we are being saved. When the Bible says salvation is *apart* from works, it is saying we cannot earn salvation by our own goodness. When the Bible says salvation must *include* works, it is telling us good works are the inevitable result of being saved.
2. This is a process. No believer becomes perfectly good all at once. We all continue to wrestle with sin, and God is always gracious and merciful in forgiving us. Our growth in obedience and good works takes time, but it does happen in every true believer's life.

So we can see, Joe, that although we do not earn our salvation through works, good works can and must mark the life of every true believer.

CAN THIS TENSION BE RESOLVED?

How shall we resolve the tension at the heart of the gospel? We can express the tension in various ways:

- Justified by faith; justified by works.
- Saved by grace; saved by obedience.
- The gospel as freedom; the gospel as law.
- The Christian as sinner; the Christian as saint.

Joe's hypothetical counselors have each tried to resolve that tension in a different way. The free salvationist has tried to deny one side of the tension altogether: Works play no role at all in anyone's salvation. By contrast, the lordship salvationist argues that a gospel of grace and a requirement for works can be reconciled. Who is right?

To my mind, only one answer is possible. The Bible clearly connects our faith with the way we live. Any attempt to deny the connection between salvation and works is profoundly misguided. So then, I suppose many would label me a lordship salvationist. With certain reservations, which should be apparent by the end of this book, I'll accept that label. If so, then what can this book add to the discussion? Do lordship salvationists need more defenders? What is left to say?

Actually, much is left to say. Acknowledging that "faith" and "works" are connected is only the beginning of the story. The most important question still remains: *How* are they connected? This is certainly Joe's question. At this point, Joe might look at the failures in his life and lament, "I'm doomed." I very much sympathize with Joe. In fact, I'm convinced that connecting faith and works in the wrong way can be worse than denying the connection at all.

But I am also convinced that the tension at the heart of the gospel can be resolved. Furthermore, it can be resolved in a way that brings out the clarity and coherence of the Bible, in a way that is intellectually satisfying, and in a way that fosters confidence and a sober joy in the Christian life. Most importantly, it can be resolved so as to speak directly to Joe's problem: He can look honestly at the very real failures in his life and still be confident that he is a child of God.

SEEING THE BIG PICTURE

The story is told of six blind men encountering an elephant. One caught hold of the tail and concluded that an elephant is like a rope. Another touched its big, broad side and decided that an elephant is like a wall. Each man felt a different part of the elephant and each drew different conclusions about elephants. In a way, anyone reading a book of theology is forced by the author to be like these blind men. The author calls the reader's attention to a particular part of the theological puzzle: "Oh, I see; it's like a rope." Then the author moves to another part of the picture, hoping the reader follows: "Wait a minute; you just said it's like a rope, but this is like a wall." All theological authors believe that the individual pieces fit together to make a coherent picture; all readers are challenging the author to prove that very point.

The rest of this book examines the puzzle of saving faith piece by piece. In other words, first we will examine the tail, then the sides, then the ears and trunk. This piecemeal approach, although necessary, can create confusion. Perhaps the reader expects the animal to look more like a giraffe than an elephant; in that case, every step of the explanation makes no sense because the reader doesn't know where the author is going. I want to try to forestall that problem. Therefore, before I go on to describe the pieces, I want to show you the whole elephant.

A very typical approach to the Bible divides its teachings into two parts: (1) those pertaining to salvation or "justification"; and (2) those pertaining to Christian growth or "sanctification." In this view, certain passages describe salvation as coming to those who believe in Jesus; certain other passages exhort us to grow in faith, wisdom, and obedience. These two kinds of passages, it is argued, have virtually nothing to do with each other. The motivation for believing is salvation; the motivation for obedience is not salvation but something else—heavenly rewards, earthly blessings, anything besides salvation.

At first this approach seems logical, and part of it is based on true biblical teaching. Justification happens at a particular point in time; sanctification works itself out over the course of a believer's life. God does not wait to forgive and justify us until we have been completely sanctified, as if sanctification were some sort of qualifying test. The youngest, rawest, most immature child of God is as secure in God's grace as the wisest and most mature saint who ever lived. In this sense, justification and sanctification can be considered as separate concepts—we can be justified before we show much evidence of being sanctified.

However, this line of thinking has not gone nearly far enough. An analogy will help make clear what I mean. Suppose my task is to find members of the oak family. An acorn, a young oak sapling, a sturdy oak tree—all of these qualify. On a certain plot of ground, a man tells me that he has planted acorns. Obviously, this is either true or not. If I were to dig one up, I would either find an acorn or something else. Its "oakness" is a settled issue. But since all the supposed acorns are under the ground, I can't know for certain now whether the man is telling the truth or not. However, if I come back years later and find that a recognizable oak tree has grown up, then I will know that, years ago, it started from a genuine acorn. Likewise, if I come back and find a tree growing lemons, I have every right to doubt that it started from an acorn at all. Nothing about its essential nature changed; the oaks were always oaks. But until they grew out of the ground enough to be recognized, I couldn't know with any certainty what they were.

The same thing is true with the children of God. We might wish that every person who believes the facts about Jesus were guaranteed to be saved, but it is not true. Saving faith arises from hearts willing to cease their rebellion against God, hearts willing to know God and themselves in a new light. People can find all kinds of reasons to "believe" while remaining hardhearted rebels against God. How then can we come to know our own hearts? We come to know them by the course our lives take. In other words:

1. We come to know that we are "justified" because we see the evidence that we are being "sanctified."

Now by itself, this statement is not nearly enough. Although it is true, it can be misunderstood and misused in terrible and destructive ways. As it stands, it might easily sound as if salvation were dependent on our moral success. You are forgiven for any sins in your past, but from now on you had better eliminate sin from your life or else you are not really a believer at all. I have a problem with that idea. For one thing, if it were true, it would disqualify me and everyone else I know from salvation. What is more relevant, such a harsh demand is far from the biblical gospel. Salvation is indeed dependent on certain things being true of us as people, but "sinlessness" would be a standard no one in this life could meet.

> 2. The children of God are "righteous sinners"; that is, although believers are still morally weak, something is distinctively right about them.

On the one hand, believers are truly sinners. For as long as we live, our lives will show an innate tendency toward evil. Neither God nor our neighbor will get from us what they deserve. Even the most mature saints, in the golden years of their walk with God, can succumb in a flash to their petty, selfish, destructive tendencies. Thus the works of believers will never be anywhere near as good as they should be in this life. I would argue that no biblical author expects his readers to escape sin and moral weakness in this lifetime; no biblical author wants our every moral failure to plunge us into doubt and despair about our own salvation. We will continue to struggle with moral failure our entire lives, and this does not call our salvation into question.

On the other hand, there is something truly right about the children of God. The hearts of believers are "good" in a way that unbelievers' aren't. That goodness consists in their willingness to accept the difficult truths about God. The gospel confronts all of us with fundamental questions about life. Among the most important are:

- Who am I? (I am an evil person who deserves God's wrath.)
- Who is God? (He is the Creator God who really exists, the One who is good and merciful and trustworthy above all others.)

■ What do I want? (I want to be freed from the curse
    that is on this world: the death, the separation from
    God, the evil around me, the evil within me, and the
    suffering all this brings.)

Do we understand all this immediately upon our conversion? Probably not. God, however, has His own ways of bringing these truths home to us.

3. God usually takes believers through a process of testing and maturing their faith, a process which shows
   the reality of His work in their hearts.
   ■ God takes us through trials that test our faith; that
     is, the trials force us to confront questions like
     "Who is God?" and "What do I want?" in real-life
     situations. When we persevere in faith, in spite of
     the pressures to bail out, we see that our hearts are
     genuinely committed to God.
   ■ The process of persevering forces us to rethink the
     questions of our faith at a deeper level. We will
     make the same choice to believe again, this time
     with more understanding of what is at stake. So
     genuine believers whose faith is tested by God will
     ultimately grow in wisdom. This wisdom is itself a
     further sign that our faith is genuine.
   ■ The end result will be "works"; that is, our lives will
     change as a result of the lessons learned through the
     testing and maturing of our faith. Since we have
     learned to answer such questions as "Who is God?"
     and "What do I want?" very differently from our
     unbelieving neighbors, certain aspects of our lives
     will show these distinctively Christian beliefs.

The single act of conversion is a promising step in a lifelong
journey, but the journey itself will tell the story. The greater the
discontinuity between what we say we believe and how we live,
the more seriously we must question whether we are in fact chil-

dren of God at all. The Bible makes it clear: Those who claim to believe and yet live stubbornly foolish and unbelieving lives raise serious questions about their salvation. Such people may in fact be believers but are immature — a stage most believers go through. But if their lives explicitly contradict what they say they believe, they cannot assume they belong to God.

In saying this, I recognize there is a potential problem. After all, none of our actions are entirely consistent with our beliefs. Paul himself describes the struggle between the good he wanted to do and the evil he did instead (Romans 7:14-25). Sin makes all of us hypocrites at times. However, the question is not whether our actions show us to be sinners. No, a trial in the biblical sense tests our *faith* and our disposition toward God and His promises. Over time, our choices show whether the gospel really means anything to us. Of course our actions show us to be sinners, but what else do they show? Are we people who know we are sinners? Have we embraced God's promises to forgive and restore us? Just as my sinfulness will show itself in my life, so also will my faith.

Like many things I am going to say in this book, what I just said needs to be clarified. I am not saying that we cannot be saved until we pass a long qualifying test. God knows our hearts from the very beginning. The thief on the cross believed and then died; this did not disqualify him from salvation, even though his faith didn't go through years of testing through trials. Our hearts are no mystery to God, but they are a mystery to us. Trials are for *our* benefit; among other things, they make the invisible realities of our own hearts visible.

What then is our motivation for heeding the exhortations and commands of the Bible? We are not earning our salvation. God is not waiting to forgive our sins until we pass the "sanctification" test. So what is at stake? The commands in the New Testament are based on one profound truth: There is a connection between our beliefs and our behavior. New Testament commands are calling us to believe the gospel again, this time with our lives instead of just our mouths. When the Bible warns us not to love money or commands us to forgive others, it is asking us to think about the truths of the gospel all over again, out in the real world with real issues on the table. How we deal with those issues says a lot about the reality going on in our hearts.

Speaking of the heart of the believer brings me to my last assertion:

> 4. There is no other source possible for the believer's new heart except God Himself. Therefore, the doctrine of election is an unavoidable part of the Bible's teaching on salvation.

I believe that God is sovereign in salvation, that He chooses who will be saved and works in their hearts to bring that salvation about. Many, I know, view this as a divisive doctrine, best left unsaid. However, I find this doctrine woven throughout all the other issues we must talk about. The last chapter explains why I think that is true. I mention it here to avoid possible misunderstanding along the way. In the pages that follow, I will sometimes speak of God's sovereign decision to save us by changing our hearts. And yet at other times I will speak of our need to "decide" or "choose" what we want and what we will do. I am not contradicting myself. No one who believes in predestination denies that human beings have real choices to make (at least, no one that I know of). I do not deny it; I affirm it — *Our destiny is based on the choices we make.* This topic will be discussed more thoroughly later. Here I only want to make it clear that I am not talking out both sides of my mouth. Like those who believe in predestination and those who do not, I believe that our choices determine our destiny. God's sovereignty does not work *in spite of* our choices or *instead of* our choices, but *through* our choices.

CONCLUSION

In the end, the dilemma of grace is no dilemma at all. The works of believers show them to be sinners, but their works also show them to be believers. God is gracious in forgiving our sins; God is also gracious in imparting, testing, and maturing the faith which marks us as His people. In the pages that follow, we will examine how the Bible speaks of these things, how they work out in life, and how important these truths are to our journey of faith.

CHAPTER TWO

Righteous Sinners

Today Joe took his Bible to work so he could study it during his lunch break. The Sermon on the Mount had always puzzled him, and he really wanted to spend time reading and thinking about it. While he pondered and prayed about these matters of eternal spiritual importance, one of his attractive female colleagues walked by. Joe began spinning out in his mind an elaborate and perverse sexual fantasy involving the woman and himself. In the middle of this reverie the phone at his desk rang. It was his wife, reminding him to come home early for a meeting at church. Joe didn't want to go to this meeting; in fact, they had fought about it the previous evening. Snared by his guilty conscience and his natural impatience, Joe snapped at his wife, leaving both of them in a foul mood as they hung up. Cursing under his breath, Joe caught sight of himself in the fake marble tile opposite his desk, his Bible still in his hand. He sat absolutely motionless for a long time, as if made of the stone himself. Then he looked down at his Bible and read through watery eyes, "Blessed are those who mourn."

Joe doesn't need to be told something is wrong with him. He can't argue with the biblical pronouncement that he is a sinner. What Joe doesn't understand is how God thinks about him. He knows that the God of the Bible is a God of love for His creation *and* of wrath against sin. Every time Joe sees moral failure in his life, he wonders whether *this* time he has shown his true colors—as an enemy of God. These words of Jesus trouble him: "So it will be at the end of the age; the angels shall come forth, and *take out the wicked from among the righteous . . .* " (Matthew 13:49). In his most fearful moments Joe says to himself, "The wicked—that must include me, right? After a day like today, how can I dare to number myself among the *righteous?*" Joe longs to know that the good news is good enough to include him.

IS JOE A RIGHTEOUS MAN?

What does the Bible mean when it speaks of the "righteous"? Although Joe does not yet feel confident as a student of the Bible, he thinks often about questions like this. A crummy day like the one he had today gives him much to think about. Vague intuitions tell him that the question of his "righteousness" is a complex one. Reflecting on the day's events, he sees several different angles from which to ask the question, "Am I a righteous man?"

One thing is clear to Joe beyond question—*He is a morally weak man.* There is no way he can claim to be righteous in the sense of "morally perfect." As he thinks back on the moral failings in his life, he knows that his stubborn selfishness was shameful and indefensible—but at the time it came to him as naturally as breathing. If the absence of sin marks the true believer, then Joe is not a believer—and he wonders if he ever could be.

A second thing also makes sense to Joe. He understands his Bible enough to know *he is a guilty man*; his conscience confirms this. Many of his friends would try to convince him that he just has a bad self-image. But he knows differently. God is holy; Joe is not. God has every right to judge and condemn Joe as a sinner.

So far, Joe can fit his experience and his theology together. He is aware of the distinction between being "made righteous" and being "declared righteous." The Cross of Christ made it possible for a sinful person—one who has not yet been *made* righteous — to be accepted by God and *declared* righteous. The gospel is about forgiveness, about being accepted in spite of our sin. Joe understands that his sin is not an obstacle to God's grace. In theory, Joe could still wrestle with sin and yet be declared "righteous" by a merciful God.

What troubles Joe, however, is the question of who *receives* this forgiveness. God's children are forgiven sinners, but aren't they more than that? The Bible seems to speak of the people of God as morally distinctive, different somehow from the godless world around them. This is the part that drives Joe crazy. How different does he have to be?

Although Joe cannot quite put the picture together yet, a third conception of "righteousness" begins to emerge in his thinking. Perhaps he might dare to hope, as he thinks about his disappointing day, that he sees signs of something right about himself. Joe doesn't quite know how to put this into words, but he hopes against hope that *he is a man with a heart for God.* The Bible describes unbelievers in various ways: stiff-necked, hard-hearted, willful, spiritually blind, and so on. Joe thinks perhaps these words don't describe him. Even on such a day of moral failure, he can see a glimmer of something encouraging about himself. He remembers that he was passionately eager to understand his Bible; he was not just reading out of a sense of religious duty. Perhaps that shows a sincere belief in the gospel. Most of all, Joe thinks about the genuine remorse he felt when he realized what he had done. He was willing to admit he had done wrong, and he sincerely longed to be a different kind of man. Jesus said, "Blessed are those who mourn"; Joe has a wild hope that maybe the fact that he mourns over his sin means he is one of those blessed ones.

RIGHTEOUSNESS IN THE BIBLE

What Joe is stumbling toward intuitively is in fact how the Bible talks about righteousness. Different issues are involved at different times. In biblical terms, the question "Am I righteous?" can mean (at least) three different things:

1. Am I morally perfect or am I morally corrupt?
2. Am I justified before God or am I condemned?
3. Does my heart respond to the truths of God or am I spiritually blind and hardhearted?

This three-fold distinction is central to the argument of this book. To give an example of how we might find this distinction at work in the Bible, we will look at Psalm 32.

Psalm 32

Psalm 32 is a psalm of David, who would have sympathized with the kind of day Joe had today. David had a day like that himself, only he went a little bit further. David actually committed adultery with the woman he lusted after, got her pregnant, and arranged for her husband to be killed. Joe's sins seem small in comparison. Yet David was called a man after God's own heart (Acts 13:22; see also 1 Kings 14:8), which should give sinners like ourselves some comfort. Perhaps it was that very sin with Bathsheba that inspired Psalm 32; whatever the specifics, clearly David was a man who knew moral failure.

> How blessed is he whose transgression is forgiven,
>   Whose sin is covered!
> How blessed is the man to whom the LORD does not
>   impute iniquity,
> And in whose spirit there is no deceit! (Psalm 32:1-2)

David grabs our attention immediately. He is talking about the good guys, the blessed ones, the people who receive God's favor. Yet—the good guys are not so good. They are transgressors, sinners, workers of iniquity. God gives them mercy, not justice. Their works are not "righteous," yet God is justifying them anyway. The apostle Paul uses David's psalm to make this very point:

> . . . just as David also speaks of the blessing upon the
>   man to whom God reckons
> righteousness apart from works:

"Blessed are those whose lawless deeds have been
    forgiven,
And whose sins have been covered.
Blessed is the man whose sin the LORD will not take into
    account." (Romans 4:6-8; quoting Psalm 32:1-2a)

Paul sees Psalm 32 as one of the classic statements in the Old Testament about justification apart from works. David is not describing a sinless person who earns God's favor; he is describing one whose sins God does not take into account.

Paul quotes only three of four poetic lines in the first two verses of Psalm 32 because they specifically deal with his topic in Romans—justification apart from works. In these first three lines, David describes the failings of this "blessed one"—he is a transgressor, a sinner, and iniquitous. David, however, goes on to say something extremely important for our topic—he describes what is *right* with the blessed one. This blessed one is different from all the *cursed* sinners in the world—he is one "in whose spirit there is no deceit." This idea of a sinner with an honest spirit is the key to understanding the psalm, and in the next section David uses his own experience as an illustration.

When I kept silent about my sin, my body wasted away
Through my groaning all day long.
For day and night Thy hand was heavy upon me;
My vitality was drained away as with the fever-heat of
    summer.
I acknowledged my sin to Thee,
And my iniquity I did not hide;
I said, "I will confess my transgressions to the LORD";
And Thou didst forgive the guilt of my sin. (Psalm 32:3-5)

To David, honesty and being forgiven go together. To have a deceitful spirit would be to lie about one's own sin, to try to deny it. An honest spirit confesses its sins to God and finds forgiveness. God's mercy covers much, but it is not unconditional: He will forgive the sinner, the transgressor, the iniquitous, but He will not forgive the self-righteous and the stubbornly dishonest.

Honesty about sin is not easy, and David struggled within himself. In the end, however, he admitted the truth to God and found forgiveness. Something is clearly wrong with David: He is a sinner. But something is right with David as well: He is honest enough to confess his sins to God and seek His mercy. David understands that he wouldn't have found God's forgiveness without such honesty. David is blessed because he is one "in whose spirit there is no deceit."

The next section of the psalm illustrates something else "right" about David: He trusts God. The question of God's forgiveness is not academic for him; he knows he needs God's forgiveness because he needs God's help. God delivers and helps His friends, those whom He has forgiven; this is David's confidence and hope.

> Therefore, let everyone who is godly pray to Thee in a
>   time when Thou mayest be found;
> Surely in a flood of great waters they shall not reach him.
> Thou art my hiding place;
> Thou dost preserve me from trouble;
> Thou dost surround me with songs of deliverance.
>   (Psalm 32:6-7)

Notice that David calls "godly" those who turn to God in confession and dependence. They are not godly in the sense of morally perfect (remember, they are sinners, transgressors, iniquitous); they are godly because they are humble and look to God for help and mercy. If we, like David, know we need God's mercy and see Him as our only hope of rescue, then we are among the godly.

In the next section of the psalm, we hear a word of warning. In Hebrew poetry, the speaker often changes without warning; we know who's talking only from the context. I take the speaker here to be God. But whether God or David is speaking, the warning remains the same:

> I will instruct you and teach you in the way which you
>   should go;

I will counsel you with My eye upon you.
Do not be as the horse or as the mule which have no
 understanding,
Whose trappings include bit and bridle to hold them in
 check,
Otherwise they will not come near to you. (Psalm 32:8-9)

Here is another vivid picture of the hearts of God's people. Those who follow God are *not* like the horse or the mule. We can get mules to do what we want, but they are not disposed by nature to do it. We have to put external controls on them to move them where we want. Some of mankind are like this. Where the things of God are concerned, they are like dumb animals who by nature do not respond to God. Of course, they cannot thwart Him. He will prevail. But their hearts do not respond to His Word and counsel. God's people are different. They seek His counsel and they want to know Him and follow Him because they trust Him.

David concludes the psalm:

Many are the sorrows of the wicked;
But he who trusts in the LORD, lovingkindness shall
 surround him.
Be glad in the LORD and rejoice, you righteous ones,
And shout for joy, all you who are upright in heart.
 (Psalm 32:10-11)

Who are the righteous ones, the upright in heart? Are they those who do not sin? No, because David is talking to sinners. David describes the "blessed ones" as honest, godly, trusting — those are the ones who are righteous and upright in heart. The wicked, in contrast, are none of these things. By "wicked" David doesn't just mean sinful; *everyone* in this psalm is sinful. The wicked are those whose spirits are dishonest and untrusting. In David's psalm we see that a person can have a bad moral character and still have a right relationship with God. But David makes it clear — one cannot have a bad spirit and have a right relationship with God. We are not blessed by God if we won't confess our sins and trust our Creator.

Distinctions in the Biblical Use of "Righteous"

The New Testament has a word for those who have the favor of God: *dikaios*. We typically translate *dikaios* (and its related forms) with words like "righteous," "just," "justified," "justification," and so on. Something is *dikaios* if it is "in the right" and therefore acceptable. Something is not *dikaios* if it is "in the wrong" and therefore to be rejected. "Rightness" and "wrongness" are the unifying ideas in all the various uses of *dikaios*. This "rightness" is crucially important because "wrongness" is the defining feature of human life. The Bible tells us—and experience confirms—that something is desperately wrong with us. Sin and its consequences are the wrong that must be put right or we perish. From the Bible's perspective, no greater calamity could fall upon us than to lack *dikaiosune*, "rightness."

In David's psalm we see three different ways in which we can talk about the "rightness" of God's people: (1) Our moral character is not "in the right"; we are sinners. (2) We have a relationship with God that is "in the right"; we are forgiven for our sins and we are "justified" apart from our works. (3) We have a spirit that is "in the right"; we are truly contrite and trust God for help and mercy. This three-fold distinction is the logic that ties Psalm 32 together; it is also at the heart of the biblical concept of "righteousness."

Having a "right" moral character. In one sense, a righteous person is anyone acceptable to God by virtue of a perfect moral character. God in His perfection must punish and reject all sin; by rights His favor belongs only to those who are completely and comprehensively good. Jesus is the only human being who has ever earned the favor of the Father on His own merits. The rest of us have no intrinsic righteousness of our own to recommend us to God.

> He saved us, not on the basis of deeds which we have done in righteousness, but according to His mercy. . . .
> (Titus 3:5)

"There is none righteous, not even one . . . there is none
who does good . . . by the works of the Law no flesh will
be justified in His sight; for through the Law comes the
knowledge of sin . . . for all have sinned and fall short of
the glory of God. . . . (Romans 3:10-23)

These verses are just two of the many that have the nature
of our moral character in view. Humanity is not righteous; we
are all sinners. God is righteous, and we ought to be like Him,
but we are not.

Having a "right" standing before God. Because we are not
good, we justly fall under the condemnation of our good and holy
Creator. If we all got what we deserved, none would survive.

If Thou, LORD, shouldst mark iniquities,
O Lord, who could stand? (Psalm 130:3)

The good news is that God has made it possible for unrighteous people to be "in the right" with Him anyway. The Cross
allows people who are *unrighteous* in character to be *righteous*
in their standing before God.

But now apart from the Law *the righteousness of God* has
been manifested, being witnessed by the Law and the
Prophets, even *the righteousness of God through faith in
Jesus Christ* for all those who believe; for there is no distinction; for all have sinned and fall short of the glory of
God, *being justified as a gift by His grace* through the
redemption which is in Christ Jesus. (Romans 3:21-24)

But to the one who does not work, but believes in *Him
who justifies the ungodly*, his faith is *reckoned as righteousness.* (Romans 4:5)

The English language sometimes uses two terms, "justification" and "righteousness," to bring out the difference in meaning: We are not righteous, but we are justified. (Although, as we

can see above, some translators use the word "righteous" to mean both, leaving the reader to sort it out.) In the original Greek, one word conveyed both meanings: We are not *dikaios* in one sense, and we are *dikaios* in another. Our moral character is not "in the right"; our standing with God is "in the right."

Having a "right" heart orientation toward God. The distinction between right moral character and right standing is clear: Believers are sinners whom God has accepted anyway. So what does Luke mean by "righteous" in the following passage?

> And behold, a man named Joseph, who was a member
> of the Council, a good and righteous man. (Luke 23:50)

Luke calls Joseph "righteous," but he doesn't mean Joseph had a flawless moral character. Neither is Luke talking about mere "justification." He is saying something positive about Joseph as a person: Joseph was a "good and righteous man." How so? Was Joseph fifty-one percent good? Was he in the top ten percent of the human race? Does God grade on the curve? In what sense was Joseph good and righteous?

We have seen the beginnings of an answer in Psalm 32. There is a sense in which the people of God are "righteous" in their spirits. Something is distinctively different about their hearts. (I am using the words "spirit" and "heart" interchangeably, just as the Bible sometimes does.) We are justified (declared righteous) by faith, but faith is the mark of a heart that has something right about it. Joseph evidently was a man after God's own heart, in spite of his human failings. He believed in and trusted God, he looked to God for mercy, and so on.

Notice carefully what I am not saying. I am not saying we are now morally perfect. I am not saying our faith earns us our salvation. I am not saying we now deserve God's blessing because we are "righteous." Our salvation is pure mercy; we do not deserve God's kindness. However, who in this life is destined to receive God's mercy? Not those who hate God. Not those who can't admit their own sin. Not those who refuse to trust God. Not the "wicked" of Psalm 32. The hearts of such people are marked. Something is fatally wrong with them: They are spiritually blind. Mercy comes to those who love God, those who know how sinful they are, those who believe God's promises, those who seek God's instruction. Their hearts are also marked. Although much is wrong with them, something is also very right: They are children of the light who have been given "eyes to see." The Bible sometimes calls them "righteous":

> And behold, there was a man in Jerusalem whose name was Simeon; and this man was *righteous and devout*, looking for the consolation of Israel; and the Holy Spirit was upon him. (Luke 2:25)

These "righteous" ones are not hypothetical, sinless people; they are flesh and blood believers. In spite of their own sinfulness, God has blessed these righteous ones with spirits alive to Him. Their hearts are rightly oriented toward God. They believe His promises and admire His goodness and lament over their own evil. Abraham's nephew Lot is a particularly interesting example of such a "righteous sinner":

> . . . *righteous* Lot, oppressed by the sensual conduct of unprincipled men (for by what he saw and heard that *righteous* man, while living among them, felt *his righteous soul* tormented day after day with their lawless deeds). . . . (2 Peter 2:7-8)

Peter calls Lot "righteous"; yet it is hard to read the story of Lot and conclude that he was an example of sinless perfection. He was a timid man with small faith. Although he believed the angels, they had to drag him out of Sodom. His daughters twice got him so drunk that he had sex with both of them and never knew it. But for all his faults, Lot was a believer in Yahweh. He cared about what was right, and he mourned over the eagerness with which Sodom gave itself over to sin.

The children of God in this life are righteous people. They are not sinless people; they do not have the righteousness of moral character that would earn them salvation. But their faith is a flag marking a certain rightness in their hearts. Unlike those in the world around them, their eyes see and their ears hear. In a blind world, such sight deserves to be called "good."

CONCLUSION

For us to make sense of the Bible and our own lives, we must understand two important truths:

1. The children of God are still morally weak and sinful.
2. The children of God are right-hearted people, with a new orientation to the truths of God.

This is one of the most important theological distinctions we can make. If we do not understand both the "rightness" and the "wrongness" of the child of God, we will consistently miss the point of much biblical teaching. We will either make the Bible say too much or too little about the nature of saving faith. This distinction is only the beginning, however. Two distinct sets of questions emerge as important:

1. What are some of these "right-hearted" qualities?
   What do they have to do with "believing in Jesus"?
2. How do these qualities show themselves in our lives?
   What is the connection between "faith" and "works"?

The next section of the book, "The Heart of the Believer," deals with the first set of questions; the second set of questions is addressed in the section after that, "Faith at Work." Together their goal is to explain why and how the Bible speaks of the Christian life the way it does.

PART TWO

THE HEART OF
THE BELIEVER

CHAPTER THREE

Who Am I?

⸺

We human beings are blind in many ways; perhaps worst of all is our inability to see the truth about ourselves. For people so addicted to the mirror, we profit from it little; we so rarely understand the person staring back at us. Of all the truths we hide from, the hard truths about ourselves are the ones we hate the most, especially the truth about our own moral unworthiness. Finding ways to justify ourselves in our own eyes is a universal pastime. Yet one of the most consistent themes in the Bible is the need for sinners to be honest about their own sin. We must ask ourselves the question "Who am I?" and we must be willing to answer it honestly.

The Bible is not just talking about how nice it would be if we confessed our sinfulness. Humble admission of our evil and guilt is not optional; it is essential. This becomes clear through three related ideas:

1. The Bible does not always describe salvation merely in terms of belief. Sometimes it presents the humble admission of our own evil and guilt as a condition for salvation.
2. A meaningful belief in Jesus must be rooted in this willingness to see our own evil and guilt. The gospel

is a rescue story, but it is hard to welcome a rescuer if you refuse to admit you are lost.

3. A person can believe without such humility, but such "faith" does not save.

The biblical teaching about humility is part of its larger teaching about the heart of the believer. As we saw in Psalm 32, the one who finds forgiveness is the one "in whose spirit there is no deceit." Jesus Himself describes true believers as "ones who have heard the word in an honest and good heart, and hold it fast, and bear fruit with perseverance" (Luke 8:15). This connection between right beliefs and a good heart is repeated throughout the Bible, which tells us that believing the gospel involves a revolution in our values, commitments, and desires. Part of the revolution in believers' hearts involves our willingness to know ourselves as the sinners we are.

We will save questions like "How does this work itself out in real life?" and "What if I fail to be as humble and contrite as I should?" for the next section of the book. Our purpose in this chapter is to make one thing very clear: A humble willingness to know ourselves as sinners is an essential part of being a believer.

What Is Sin?

If honesty about our sins is so important, then we had better be clear about what we mean by "sin." Our culture has trivialized the word "sin." Anyone worried about sin must be a hateful, self-righteous prude pointing the finger at others and saying, "Repent, you sinners!" Our culture's real attitude toward sin is seen in our candy bar commercials, where half-dressed women purr over their chocolate, "It's sinfully delicious." This is tragic because the word "sin" should conjure up very different images. Sin is our great problem, burden, enemy, tragedy, and disease.

People are inclined to reserve the word "sin" for major offenses like murder, theft, and adultery. By that standard, it is easy for many to dismiss the idea that they are sinners. But the

Bible sees the problem of sin as a problem of the heart. At heart, human beings are rebels against goodness, and that is true for everybody—murderers and non-murderers alike. The "big" sins get our attention because of their dramatic consequences in the world. But Jesus made it clear: A heart filled with hate is evil, whether or not that hate turns into murder. The mind indulging itself in evil fantasies is corrupt, whether or not those fantasies get acted out in adultery.

A good way to understand the magnitude of our sin problem is to think about its opposite. What would a healthy, sinless humanity look like? Jesus summed it up by reminding us of the two great commandments: Love God and love your neighbor (Matthew 22:35-40). Love of God and love of neighbor are right and good. People who love in this way have accepted the truth about who God is, who their neighbors are, and (very importantly) who they themselves are. God is wise and good, and we all are His creatures. God deserves all our love, loyalty, and gratitude; our neighbor, our fellow creature, deserves just as much consideration as we do. People who love in this way see the world the way it is. God is in His rightful place of central importance, and we, His creatures, are arrayed around Him, none more prominent than another, like planets dancing obediently around a blazing sun.

Unfortunately, our view of ourselves is as distorted as Ptolemy's belief that the sun traveled around the earth. All of us, by nature, believe ourselves to be at the center of our own universe—with God and everyone else in orbit around us. We don't conclude this after reflecting on our experience; we are born believing it is true. Our own desires are much more important than our Creator's desires or other people's desires. We believe this fiercely and instinctively, the way we believe in gravity. When we feel our desires being thwarted, our gut reaction is as natural and quick as when we feel ourselves falling: We don't want to fall, and we don't want our desires thwarted. In our twisted set of values, neither God nor our neighbor is as important as ourselves.

To admit that we are sinners, therefore, is to admit that the fundamental stance of our lives, the basic tendency of our hearts, is wrong. Even on our best days, we treat God with a neglect bordering on contempt. Even on our best days, our thoughts are riveted on our own needs at the expense of others. (Ask the AIDS volunteer who sulks all day because someone took her parking place.) Yes, we are capable of a kind of love, but we have given neither God nor our neighbor the love they deserve. We are wrapped up in ourselves, which is the very essence of sin. R. C. Sproul calls it "cosmic treason." We are in revolt against our rightful place in the universe. This is the truth about ourselves that God asks us to admit when we hear the gospel.

THE PHARISEE AND THE TAX GATHERER

In the previous chapter we discussed Psalm 32, a wonderful meditation on the need for humble honesty before God. The Bible's greatest teaching on this theme, however, is Jesus' parable of the Pharisee and the tax gatherer.

We will misunderstand the impact of this story unless we get the characters straight. This is a story about two stock characters in Jewish life. In our terms, one wears a white cowboy hat, and the other a long black cloak and curly black mustache. In our time we so commonly use the word "Pharisee" as a term of derision that we might miss the turnaround Jesus makes. Jesus' listeners, however, understood the Pharisee to be a model of godly devotion, and they would have had nothing but contempt for the tax gatherer, a fellow Jew who collected taxes for the Roman conquerors. After paying Rome what he owed it, the tax gatherer could keep the rest of what he collected. Nothing stopped him from imposing a great tax burden on the people and keeping a big chunk for himself. A tax gatherer was a corrupt official, a traitor, and an oppressor. He was the bitter human form the Roman conquest took in every Jew's life—the Roman oppression with a Jewish face. People hated him.

So in Jesus' parable, when the Pharisee and the tax gatherer went to the temple to pray, the Pharisee's prayer makes some sense: "God, I thank Thee that I am not like other people: swindlers, unjust, adulterers, or even like this tax-gatherer. I fast twice a week; I pay tithes of all that I get" (Luke 18:11-12). Much of what he says is probably true. Undoubtedly he never has committed adultery or extortion, and he does keep the requirements of the law as he understands them. If you compare his actions with those of the tax collector, there is no question who is the more model citizen, who has walked the straighter path. And in his words at least, the Pharisee does not take credit for this himself. He "humbly" thanks God for making him better than others. Only one thing is wrong with what he says: He is self-deceived. He is just as much a sinner—just as much a failure at loving God and man—as the tax gatherer. Just because he has managed to avoid the more public and unpopular sins, he believes this makes him a better person *at heart*. This is a profound misunderstanding, an audacious self-deception. Whatever the tax gatherer's faults may be, he at least has learned the truth about himself:

> "But the tax gatherer, standing some distance away, was even unwilling to lift up his eyes to heaven, but was beating his breast, saying, 'God, be merciful to me, the sinner!' I tell you, this man went down to his house justified rather than the other; for every one who exalts himself shall be humbled, but he who humbles himself shall be exalted." (Luke 18:13-14)

The tax man is a contemptible sinner, but unlike the Pharisee, he knows it. He can't thank God for making him so great, for he knows better. He can only beg God for mercy; he can only hope God will show him a kindness he doesn't deserve. And God grants him that kindness. God accepts the despicable tax collector and rejects the "godly" Pharisee.

This parable gives us an amazing and unexpected insight into the mind of God. All of us tend to think that "good people" deserve better somehow than "bad people," but in this story

God rejects the good guy and embraces the bad guy. Even we Christians, whose theology tells us that salvation comes by faith, can't help feeling that people who do the right thing deserve more from God than people who mess up. But God offers only two options, neither of which is intuitively obvious to us: either *justice*, which condemns all of us (even the most straight-shooting) as selfish, sinful people, or *mercy*, which freely accepts even the most morally repulsive of us. The children of light and the children of darkness do not necessarily differ in how far they have fallen; they differ, among other things, in the honesty with which they see their fall.

We should not downplay the issue involved in this parable: Nothing less than these men's eternal destiny is at stake. The tax gatherer comes seeking mercy from God; if he does not receive mercy, then he knows he stands condemned before a righteous God. Jesus says he received that mercy; that is, he "went down to his house justified." Conversely, the proud Pharisee went home unjustified. This fits everything we know Jesus taught about the Pharisees. Jesus comments elsewhere that those Pharisees who had such attitudes were "whitewashed tombs." A clean white veneer covered the death and decay of pride and contemptuous self-righteousness. They took pride in their outwardly "good" (of a sort) behavior and denied the worldliness and rebellion within. Jesus condemns them in the strongest possible language, saying, "How shall you escape the sentence of hell?" (Matthew 23:33). The kingdom of God, which the Pharisees expected to enter as their due, would be closed to them.

The New Testament does not attempt to paint the whole picture of salvation in any one place. In the parable of the Pharisee and the Tax gatherer, Jesus focuses tightly on one issue: an honest admission of our guilt before God. He does not talk about the cross nor urge us to believe the gospel. This does not mean that He sees those things as unimportant, only that He intends to highlight one important truth. When we step back and look at the larger biblical picture, we see that the humble honesty pictured in the parable is a necessary accompaniment to faith.

To believe the gospel, to accept Jesus as our Messiah, we have to be willing to be exposed as the sinners we are. Many are uncomfortable with Jesus precisely because they don't want to be honest about their own sin. Jesus makes this point explicitly to His brothers:

> "The world cannot hate you; but it hates Me, because I testify of it, that its deeds are evil." (John 7:7)

The world hates Jesus because He reminds it of an offensive truth. The gospel is good news, but it is *hard* news as well. The gospel tells us how God sees us. After all, at the center of the gospel is a cross, and Jesus didn't hang there because *He* deserved it. *My* sins made the cross necessary. The humiliation of Jesus on the cross is not really His; it is mine. To believe the gospel, I must accept willingly the verdict of God on my life.

PAUL ON FAITH AND SELF-RIGHTEOUSNESS

No one is more of a champion for "justification by faith" than Paul. Yet in the very writings most devoted to that topic, Romans and Galatians, he makes it clear that belief does not stand alone. Belief is rooted in the honesty to admit that we are condemned sinners. A "faith" without such humility, he argues, is not saving faith. The great error Paul fights in these letters is self-righteousness; that is, the arrogant denial of our own guilt, the mistaken belief that God accepts us because of our good behavior.

Paul wrote the book of Romans to defend his gospel against the charges of Jewish unbelievers. Part of Romans elaborates on the *reason* the Jews rejected Jesus. Romans 9–11 says that the majority of Jews did not believe the gospel because their hearts had been hardened against it. Paul specifically tells us the nature of that hardness:

> Israel, pursuing a law of righteousness, did not arrive at that law. Why? Because they did not pursue it by faith,

but as though it were by works. . . . They have a zeal for
God, but not in accordance with knowledge. For not
knowing about God's righteousness, and seeking to
establish their own, they did not subject themselves to
the righteousness of God. (Romans 9:31-32, 10:2-3)

Paul's Jewish opponents rejected his gospel because of their
essential self-righteousness. They were not interested in the
gospel; the gospel was about undeserved mercy. Instead, they
wanted to believe that their obedience to the Jewish law earned
them God's favor. If they believed the gospel, they would have
to believe that they were no better than any Gentile sinner. As
Paul makes clear in Romans 2, his opponents were characterized
by a self-righteous judgmentalism that looked down on pagan
lawbreakers, even as these legalists denied their own guilt before
God. To avoid God's judgment, they would need to repent and
seek God's mercy.

For Paul's Jewish detractors, therefore, disbelief in the
gospel was not just a factual mistake; it was an indicator of a
spiritual disease. Likewise, belief in the gospel is an indicator
that the spiritual disease has been healed. Thus we see in
Romans what we have seen in the teaching of Jesus: Unbelief
is rooted in hatred of the truth—in this case, the truth about
one's essential unworthiness before God. Believers are willing
to know themselves as sinners in need of mercy; that's partly
why they believe.

The Faith That Doesn't Save
In Romans, Paul is fighting Jewish legalists who refuse to
believe the gospel because of self-righteousness. Their unbelief is rooted in their vain attempt to justify themselves
through keeping the law. This raises an interesting question.
Can a self-righteous person still believe the gospel story? If
so, is such "belief" worthy to be called saving faith? The book
of Galatians helps us answer these questions, and in the
process it gives us a valuable clarification of what Paul means
by "justification by faith."

In Galatians, Paul is dealing with a different kind of problem from the one in Romans. He is battling the Judaizers, of whom we catch a glimpse in Acts 15:

> And some men came down [to Antioch] from Judea and began teaching the brethren, "Unless you are circumcised according to the custom of Moses, you cannot be saved." And when Paul and Barnabas had great dissension and debate with them, the brethren determined that Paul and Barnabas . . . should go up to Jerusalem to the apostles and elders concerning this issue. . . . And when they arrived at Jerusalem, they . . . reported all that God had done with them. But *certain ones of the sect of the Pharisees who had believed*, stood up, saying, "It is necessary to circumcise them, and to direct them to observe the Law of Moses." (Acts 15:1-5)

Most Pharisees (like those Paul refutes in Romans) remained stubbornly insistent that Jesus was *not* the Messiah—most, but not all. Some Pharisees "believed." In the context of Acts we know what this means. They heard the apostles' teaching that Jesus is the Christ whom God raised from the dead, and they believed it. However, some of those believing Pharisees retained the same attitude toward the Jewish law that they had always had: God is pleased with those who keep the Jewish regulations, and He rejects those who break them. This is the teaching that Paul is fighting in Galatians.

Because the issue in Galatians is different from the issue in Romans, the way Paul speaks of faith and the gospel is different as well. Unlike his letter to the Romans, Paul does not describe the message to be believed simply in terms of Christ's resurrection; all parties in the Galatians debate agreed that Jesus was the resurrected Christ. In Romans, self-righteous attitudes about the law *kept* the Jews from believing Jesus was the Christ; but in Galatians, self-righteous attitudes about the law were *added* to belief that Jesus was the Christ. But justification is not possible for those who self-righteously believe they can earn God's favor; it doesn't matter whether they believe Jesus is the Christ or not. The entire argument of Galatians supports this, but three of Paul's points are particularly worth noting:

1. Paul calls the teaching of the Judaizers "a different gospel": I am amazed that you are so quickly deserting Him who called you by the grace of Christ, for a different gospel; which is really not another; only there are some who are disturbing you, and want to distort the gospel of Christ. But even though we, or an angel from heaven, should preach to you a gospel contrary to that which we have preached to you, let him be accursed. (Galatians 1:6-8)

   Adding "you must earn your salvation through law-keeping" to the message "Jesus is the Christ" creates something that is not the gospel at all. It becomes a message that a self-righteous heart can believe, and no one will find favor with God without abandoning self-righteousness. Even though the Judaizers are described in Acts as having "believed," Paul does not hesitate to call them "accursed." We should not minimize this curse. These men have distorted Paul's message beyond recognition. They believe and teach a gospel that Paul says cannot save anyone. There can be no question that the curse Paul calls down on them involves anything less than their eternal destiny.

2. When Peter mistakenly accommodates the Judaizers Paul says Peter is "not straightforward about the truth of the gospel" (Galatians 2:14). In other words, although Paul often describes the gospel as "Jesus is the Christ who rose from the dead," there is potentially more to the gospel. In this case, the "truth of the gospel" is not about the resurrection; it is about sin, about the impossibility of pleasing God through law-keeping, about undeserved grace. The Judaizers rejected this clear implication of the

gospel, showing that their hearts were still hardened against the truths of God, *even though* they accepted Jesus as the Messiah.

3. Paul tells the Galatians: If you receive circumcision, Christ will be of no benefit to you. And I testify again to every man who receives circumcision, that he is under obligation to keep the whole Law. (Galatians 5:2-3)

To believe the message about Jesus is not enough; the Judaizers needed to reject the lie that they could please God through their law-keeping. Although they retain their belief in Jesus as the Messiah, He "will be of no benefit" to them; they have believed in the wrong Jesus, a fictitious Messiah they themselves created.

Paul's argument in Galatians is tremendously important because it clarifies his view of "justification by faith." In Romans, Paul can say we are justified through belief that Jesus is the resurrected Christ, and as far as it goes this is true. However, if we insist on clinging to the falsehood that we can please God through our law-keeping, then we are not saved, *whether we believe Jesus is the Christ or not.* Only a faith that is an expression of genuine humility before God will save us; a belief in the doctrines about Jesus without that humility will save nobody.

CONCLUSION

The Bible does not merely present "belief in Jesus" as the requirement for salvation:

1. It also ties our salvation to our willingness to acknowledge our own guilt.
2. This only makes sense since faith in Jesus is intimately connected with our willingness to admit our need for mercy.
3. It is possible to believe the basic doctrines about Jesus without actually having such humility; this kind of "belief" will not save anyone.

We have many questions left to answer about how all this works itself out in the Christian life, and we will do so in later chapters. What is important now is that we understand how important humility is to our eternal destiny. Self-righteousness is one of the most terrible of all spiritual diseases. Jesus and Paul attack self-righteousness with great power in their most important teachings. Those who enter the kingdom of God will be those who admit that they have no right to be there.

CHAPTER FOUR

Who is God?

Humanity has always put God on trial. Does He exist? If He does, why doesn't He solve my problems? Can He defend Himself for having created such a messed-up world? Many people (and I used to be among them) contend that they will only believe in God if He proves His existence and defends Himself against many serious charges. One of the striking things about those who believe in Jesus is that they do not share this attitude toward God. In their minds the positions have reversed: God is not the defendant; He is the judge. His character is not in question; ours is. The Bible makes it quite clear that those who inherit salvation have a new attitude toward God.

Since most believers have probably struggled with their attitude toward God at times, the assertions of this chapter may be somewhat unsettling. I am not denying that genuine believers can and do wrestle with God; such wrestling is a natural part of the journey. Later chapters will make this clear, I hope. What I want to make clear now, however, is that the Bible does not separate belief in the gospel from our attitude toward God. We believe the gospel because we are willing to know God; a belief in the gospel apart from such willingness is not saving faith.

FAITH AND THE KNOWLEDGE OF GOD

We call the story of God's dealing with us a "gospel," good news, glad tidings. What God has promised to do for us in Christ (which we will explore in the next chapter) is good beyond measure, so good we cannot take it all in. This picture of abundant generosity is hard to reconcile with our natural suspicion of God. To embrace the gospel means we must abandon our mistrust of God and recognize Him for His kindness, His generosity, and His trustworthiness.

A well-known verse from Hebrews provides one powerful example:

And without faith it is impossible to please Him, for he who comes to God must believe that He is, and that He is a rewarder of those who seek Him. (Hebrews 11:6)

To understand this deceptively simple verse, we must step back to remind ourselves what the book of Hebrews is about. One purpose informs the letter from beginning to end: To warn its readers not to abandon their belief that Jesus is the Christ. At stake is their eternal destiny.

For this reason we must pay much closer attention to what we have heard, lest we drift away from it. . . . How shall we escape if we neglect so great a salvation? (Hebrews 2:1,3)

Anyone who has set aside the Law of Moses dies without mercy on the testimony of two or three witnesses. How much severer punishment do you think he will deserve who has trampled under foot the Son of God, and has regarded as unclean the blood of the covenant by which he was sanctified, and has insulted the Spirit of grace? For we know Him who has said, "Vengeance is Mine, I will repay." (Hebrews 10:28-30)

Hebrews 11:6 is part of the chapter in which the author argues that believing the gospel is essentially the same kind of "faith" that the Old Testament saints demonstrated. The New Testament believer faces the sort of choice that the Old Testament believer did: Faith has always been the only way to please God. We cannot minimize what "pleasing God" means. In Hebrews, the one who pleases God inherits eternal life; the one who does not is lost. We can see this in the verses leading up to Hebrews 11:

> "But My righteous one shall live by faith; And if he shrinks back, My soul has no pleasure in him." But we are not of those who shrink back to destruction, but of those who have faith to the preserving of the soul. (Hebrews 10:38-39)

Believers are those who "live," who "preserve their souls," because God is pleased with them; they persevere in their faith and do not shrink back. God is displeased with those without this faith, and their end is destruction. As the readers of Hebrews stand on the verge of turning away from Jesus, they risk losing their souls in the cataclysmic displeasure of God. That is the background to the words of Hebrews 11:6, "without faith it is impossible to please Him. . . . " Everyone who turns away from the truth of God in unbelief comes under the divine displeasure, and without God's favor we are lost.

Now we are in a position to understand Hebrews 11:6. The readers must not turn away from Jesus in unbelief because without faith it is impossible to please God. Why? Because "faith" involves accepting two fundamental truths about God.

1. Those who are pleasing to God must believe that He exists.
2. Those who are pleasing to God must believe that He rewards those who seek Him. In other words, they must believe that He is good, trustworthy, and generous. They must understand that God knows what is

good for us and that He is willing to give it to us. They believe God's promises because they do not share the rest of mankind's suspicion and hostility toward God; they know He is to be trusted.

If we don't pay close attention to the context of Hebrews 11, the word "reward" could be misleading. Some Christians look beyond their hope of eternal life to additional "rewards" for their faithfulness. That is not what Hebrews 11:6 is talking about. The chapter repeatedly connects the hope of the Old Testament saints with that of New Testament believers. We and they are looking for the same promise: the city with foundations, the heavenly country — eternal life in the kingdom of God.

The importance of Hebrews 11:6 is the connection it implies between faith in Jesus and an understanding of God. If the readers turn away from the gospel in unbelief, they will not just be getting a theological doctrine wrong. They are turning a deaf ear to a message from God Himself because they have lost confidence that He is trustworthy. According to this verse, faith cannot be reduced to doctrinal correctness; faith is a willingness to believe God because we know that He exists and is our true and trustworthy source of what is good.

Hebrews 10:23 tells us, "Let us hold fast the confession of our hope without wavering, for He who promised is faithful." "Wavering" is exactly what the readers of Hebrews are doing. A few more steps, and they will cross the line into open rebellion against the gospel. The author of Hebrews is urging them to hold fast to the gospel, to the message of hope to be found in Jesus. Belief in Jesus, however, is built on the foundation of the trustworthiness of God. Hebrews 10:23 shows us the inevitable progression: Christian belief stands on a great hope; that hope is founded on a promise; and that promise is built solidly on the faithful character of God. The gospel can't mean anything to us if we don't know God. We have to know that He exists and that He is good and trustworthy above everything and everyone else in this world.

The readers of Hebrews were obviously vacillating in their belief in Jesus. This struggle by itself does not prove them to be unbelievers. But the author of Hebrews was warning them: The choice to believe in Jesus is the choice to know and trust God; if we refuse to know God, we are turning our backs on eternal life.

FEARING GOD

Psalm 111:10 reminds us that "the fear of the Lord is the beginning of wisdom." Fear of God is a consistent biblical theme, yet the concept of fearing God is not popular among some groups of Christians today. We would like to picture God as our daddy, our friend, our biggest fan. Certainly, these images capture something of God's tremendous love and mercy. However, even in the New Testament, which emphasizes God's grace, the same theme emerges: The people of God are those who fear Him.

> Now there was a certain man at Caesarea named Cornelius . . . a devout man, and *one who feared God* with all his household, and gave many alms to the Jewish people, and prayed to God continually. . . . And they said, "Cornelius, a centurion, a righteous and *God-fearing man*. . . . Peter said: "I most certainly understand now that God is not one to show partiality, but in every nation *the man who fears Him and does what is right, is welcome to Him.* (Acts 10:1-2,22,34-35)

As a Jew, Peter shared the Jewish perception that the kingdom of God belonged to the Jews; they were God's chosen people, and they kept His law. But Peter had to unlearn everything he had thought about the Gentiles. God called him to preach the gospel to the household of Cornelius, to tell them that those who believe in Jesus find forgiveness of sins. When God pours out His Spirit on these Gentiles, Peter realized that God has accepted them. Peter described their "welcome" in terms of their "fear" of God, not (as we might expect) in terms of their belief.

But what does it mean to fear God? It helps to compare "the fear of God" with another biblical concept, "the fear of men." To fear men means to recognize the power that human beings have to help or to harm me in this life; to fear men is to submit to others out of fear of what they might do. We all find it easy to fear men; experience teaches us the pain that human beings can inflict on each other. Unfortunately, our fear of men makes it easy to ignore God. When people disapprove of us the consequences are immediate. In comparison, God's displeasure seems intangible and remote, which is why to be a person who fears God instead of men is so significant. Fearing God means seeing God, not man, as the power to be dealt with, the one whose goodwill we must not lose.

> "And I say to you, My friends, do not be afraid of those who kill the body, and after that have no more that they can do. But I will warn you whom to fear: fear the One who after He has killed has authority to cast into hell; yes, I tell you, fear Him!" (Luke 12:4-5)

To fear God is to know Him and to understand the seriousness of our situation before Him. In Luke, Jesus calmly tells us that we can safely ignore our fellow men since the worst they can do is murder us. Murder insignificant? Yes. Compared to our eternal destiny, murder is insignificant. God is our Creator and righteous Judge, and so His good opinion is more precious than the united approval of all mankind. Jesus is urging us to ask: "Who is the most dangerous? If we have to make someone unhappy, whom should we choose?" The wise person will fear God and ignore the disapproval of the world.

Of course, the mere fact that someone takes a "me against the world" attitude is not proof of genuine belief. Without the humble confession of our own failures, without a commitment to love and mercy, we can too easily turn into self-made martyrs. Some religious zealots deserve the disapproval that the world gives them. However, Jesus is very clear that the choice to be a humble believer involves choosing whom to fear.

One last qualification is important: Fearing God is not the same as being afraid. Believers are not being asked to live in a constant state of abject terror, to live with the panicky, terrified feeling that we are doomed. We have been forgiven; we have been accepted. This kind of fear is banished by the gospel, as Paul tells us:

> For you have not received a spirit of slavery leading to
> fear again, but you have received a spirit of adoption as
> sons by which we cry out, "Abba! Father!" (Romans 8:15)

If we were dependent on earning our salvation through our own worthiness, then terror would truly be appropriate. But the news is good: No longer unworthy slaves, believers have been adopted as sons. The gospel frees us from the sickening fear of rejection that comes from knowing our own unworthiness. Still, we know that nothing but the mercy of God stands between us and condemnation. God's merciful good opinion of us is more precious than anything man could give us or take from us. In that sense we fear God more than man. We can see this balance between encouragement and fear in Acts 9:

> So the church throughout all Judea and Galilee and
> Samaria enjoyed peace, being built up; and, going on in
> the fear of the Lord and in the comfort of the Holy
> Spirit, it continued to increase. (Acts 9:31)

God's Spirit is building us up with comfort and encouragement, not tearing us down with terror. Even so, our faith is always standing on the foundation of a righteous fear of God.

LOVING GOD

> And we know that God causes all things to work
> together for good *to those who love God*, to those who are
> called according to His purpose. (Romans 8:28)

> But just as it is written,
> "Things which eye has not seen and ear has not heard,

And which have not entered the heart of man,
All that God has prepared *for those who love Him*."
(1 Corinthians 2:9)

Listen, my beloved brethren: did not God choose the
poor of this world to be rich in faith and heirs of the
kingdom which He promised *to those who love Him*?
(James 2:5)

Note that the promises in the verses above are not made to
"those who believe in Jesus" but to "those who love God." To
know whether or not we are people who love God, we need to
understand how the Bible is using the word "love." The idea of
"loving God" can easily be misunderstood. We might assume that
if we get worked up emotionally about God, we are people who
love Him. This is as fallacious as thinking that married love is the
same as those wild emotions we call "being in love." Equating an
emotional experience with "loving God" can lead us astray. The
depth of one's love of God is not measured by the number of tis-
sues used at the worship service. People who don't love God (in
the biblical sense) can have powerful religious experiences; people
who do love God don't experience an unending emotional high.
Emotions play a big part in human life. They play a part in marriage; they play a part in loving God. In each case, however, the
"love" required is a more profound commitment of the heart.

Sometimes it helps to see how a word is used when con-
trasted with its opposite. In particular, the biblical authors often
contrast "love" with "hate":

"He who loves his life loses it; and he who hates his life
in this world shall keep it to life eternal." (John 12:25)

If we think of "love" and "hate" simply in terms of emotional
states, what Jesus says here makes no sense. If we are feeling good
about our lives—say we are feeling the joy of new parenthood—
are we then destined for damnation? On the other hand, if we are
morose and suicidal, does this qualify us for salvation? Obviously

"love" and "hate" have a different sense here. The issue is whether we see our lives in this age as our prize, our treasure to guard above all else. If we look at life in this evil age and say, "This is good enough; this is what I want," then we "love" our lives. On the other hand, if we see the kingdom of God as our prize, then we "hate" our lives now. We will not sacrifice anything of eternal importance to keep this life because we "love" the next one.

Elsewhere Jesus makes the same interesting love/hate distinction:

> "No servant can serve two masters; for either he will hate the one, and love the other, or else he will hold to one, and despise the other. You cannot serve God and mammon." (Luke 16:13)

This passage tells us that when we have two competing interests, like God and mammon (wealth), we serve the one we "love," the one worthy of our service, the one whose mastery will be best for us in the end. Our "love" is not an emotional state, although it is often accompanied by a variety of emotions. What we "love" is what we treasure and desire, that to which we are committed above all else. To love God is to treasure His character, His mercy, and His promises.

Ultimately we can't embrace the gospel without loving God. The gospel is all about His goodness (and our evil), His mercy, and His deliverance. If we don't see ourselves in need of goodness, mercy, and deliverance, then the gospel can't mean much to us. The gospel shows us that God is everything we are not but want to be; He can do everything we cannot do for ourselves. He is our Creator and our Deliverer. We cling to Him as the One whom we must not lose; we love Him.

CONCLUSION

In the previous chapter we saw that the Bible characterizes the people of God in more ways than just "believing in Jesus." Those who are saved are those who humbly acknowledge their own guilt. In this chapter we see another truth about God's people: They trust God as the giver of life, fear Him as their judge, and love Him as the model and source of all that life should be. It only makes sense that this would be true. Jesus Himself connects our attitude toward Jesus with our attitude toward the Father:

> "He who believes in Me does not believe in Me, but in Him who sent Me." (John 12:44)

> "He who hates Me hates My Father also." (John 15:23)

As with the last chapter, we are left with many questions about how these things work themselves out in the Christian life, questions still to be addressed. Here, however, we have a developing picture of what it means to be a person of faith. Faith is more than a one-time act of changing our doctrinal opinions; faith is an expression of a heart willing to know the truth—in this case, the truth about God. One of the issues on which our destiny hangs is our willingness to know God as He is.

CHAPTER FIVE

What Do I Want?

⟡

At this moment, all over the world, thousands of waitresses are asking the most important question anyone will ever ask, "And you, *what do you want*?" We are creatures of desire, and, since we can't have everything, we are constantly required to choose. The waitress, of course, is asking me to make a fairly trivial choice; if I don't have the lasagna today, I can always have it next time. Other choices, like whether to marry, unalterably affect the course of our entire lives. We sculpt our lives, carving away the excess to leave what we think essential. Every truly signifi-cant choice we make requires us to reject some things in order to embrace others.

We may not be used to thinking about faith as a choice between competing desires, but the Bible presents it in exactly that way. On one side is "the world"; on the other are the promises of God. Which means more to us? We have already seen that belief in the gospel involves asking questions like "Who am I?" and "Who is God?" But no one can come to terms with the gospel without confronting the additional, very personal question, "What do I want?"

As in the last two chapters, my main purpose is to show that "faith" cannot be separated from certain fundamental heart issues. Specifically, the true child of God is one whose heart longs for what God has promised in the gospel. The latter part of this chapter will look at two passages that demonstrate how our faith and our desires are connected. It would be unwise, however, to assume that we all agree on what the gospel promises and why it is so valuable. The first part of the chapter, therefore, will explore the nature of our hope as believers.

HOPE FOR THE FUTURE

The gospel is a story told to us by God, and part of that story is God's promise to give His people great things. To understand this promise, however, we must sort out how much it represents a future hope and how much a present reality. Christians do not always agree about this. As a young Christian, I picked up from other Christians that thinking too much about the afterlife is not "cool." Only naïve, "pie in the sky" Christians got worked up about the return of Jesus. Obviously, if Christianity was going to prove itself worthy of being taken seriously, it would have to demonstrate its benefits in *this life*, or what good was it? This sounded reasonable — for a while. However, I soon discovered a collection of extremely "pie in the sky" Christian writings: the Bible.

The Bible's overriding message is that the Christian life is one of hope. As believers, we persevere in our journey down an often difficult road because our eyes are fixed on the Promised Land. No message can claim to be biblical and downplay the central role of our hope in the Christian life. If we are not living our lives today with our hearts firmly set on our glorious inheritance, we have missed the point of much the Bible teaches. To make this clear, I have paraphrased the message of several important texts:

> It may not seem like it, but it is a great thing to be hated by unbelievers for your faith. Be glad to share in the persecution of the prophets today so you can share in the reward of the prophets tomorrow. (Matthew 5:10-12)

You can protect nothing in this life from the ravages of time or the deceit of men. Store your valuables in heaven, where they cannot decay or be stolen. (Matthew 6:19-21)

The life you have now is not even worthy to be called your real life; your real life is hidden with Christ. When He returns in all His glory, your life will be revealed with Him. (Colossians 3:1-4)

This age is a time of suffering for the people of God; we suffer with Christ in order that we may share His glory when He returns. Today's sufferings dwindle into insignificance when we compare them with what God has prepared for us. Remember, this is the time of groaning. We do not yet have what we most want and need; that is why we have a "hope" and not an "accomplished fact." (Romans 8:17-25)

We must make the same choice the Old Testament saints did. They suffered and died without receiving what God had promised, but they looked past their shaky lives in this world to a city with an unshakable foundation. Our situation is the same; we must hold fast to our faith like runners in an endurance race, setting our eyes on the finish line, so that we and the saints of old may share the prize together. (see Hebrews 11)

Think of your life now as being like the labors of the farmer in the field. The work is hard, dirty, and long, but the farmer patiently endures it all because he expects a harvest. The coming of Jesus is our harvest, the great hope which inspires us to endure our troubles patiently now. (James 5:7-8)

What has God done for His children? He has given us a living hope, an imperishable inheritance reserved for us in the heavenly places, a salvation which will be revealed when Jesus returns. This hope gives us joy in the midst of the distressing trials of this age. So then, don't let the distractions of this world get you drunk; stay sober by setting your hope completely on the return of Jesus and the gracious inheritance He brings. (1 Peter 1:3-13)

I could quote many more passages, from both Testaments, to make the same point. To be a believer is a blessed thing, but not because this life is totally satisfying or free from suffering. We are blessed because a great inheritance awaits us.

The criticism that some people are "so heavenly minded that they are no earthly good" is not totally invalid. Some Christians, foolishly treating the prophetic details in the Bible like a puzzle to be solved, are so preoccupied with the "where" and the "when" that they lose sight of the "so what?" However, the Bible does call us to a wise preoccupation with the future. The crown of righteousness will be given to "all who have loved His appearing" (2 Timothy 4:8). The true Christian hope does not make us "no earthly good"; those with this hope are the most earthly good:

But the day of the Lord will come like a thief, in which the heavens will pass away. . . . Since all these things are to be destroyed in this way, *what sort of people ought you to be in holy conduct and godliness*, looking for and hastening the coming of the day of God . . . ? (2 Peter 3:10-12)

We know that, when He appears, we shall be like Him, because we shall see Him just as He is. And *everyone who has this hope fixed on Him purifies himself*, just as He is pure. (1 John 3:2-3)

The Christian hope, as the Bible portrays it, is meant to be the driving force of our lives—to inspire us to follow goodness and to provide the basis for contentment in a broken and unsatisfying world. This idea is not well understood, however, in part because we don't understand *why* the Christian hope is so valuable. We turn our attention to that question next.

FROM DEATH TO LIFE

I have noticed that, when many Christians speak of their hope for the future, they present a bland picture hardly recognizable from a biblical perspective. They typically say something like, "When we die, we will go to heaven. We will see our loved ones, we will praise Jesus all day long, and we will be happy." Sometimes they themselves admit that this picture is uninspiring. Many loved ones (the unbelieving ones) will not be in heaven. They can't imagine how praising Jesus could be interesting for more than a day or so, much less for eternity. And they can't imagine being happy in the absence of everything they have enjoyed in this life. These Christians are right to wonder if "heaven" is all there is because their picture of life after death has not even scratched the surface of all that comprises the Christian hope.

It's significant that the Bible very rarely describes the Christian hope as "When I die I'll go to heaven." Although a few passages seem to imply this picture, the meaning of those passages is debated. When the Bible speaks of the Christian hope, it almost always speaks of the second coming of Christ, the time when Jesus returns to the earth. Paul speaks of "the blessed hope and appearing of the glory of our great God and Savior, Christ Jesus" (Titus 2:13). This is not the message of a few verses, but the overwhelming testimony of the New Testament. Why? Why should the return of Christ be the great guiding star for believers?

To understand how desirable Christ's return is, we need to think about the human condition. What is our problem? What could make human life completely fulfilling and satisfying? The answer may not be intuitively obvious, but the Bible asserts that the great enemies of human fulfillment are the curse of sin and the futility of death.

The Wages of Sin

From the beginning, the Bible clearly shows sin to be mankind's tragic and fatal flaw. One of the strong themes of the Old Testament is the corruption of Adam and Eve's children: brother kills brother; God sends a flood because every thought of man's heart "was only evil continually"; a mob of men try to rape angels; the story goes on and on. The history of Israel is largely a history of moral failure—a sobering story of idolatry, betrayal, adultery, greed, disobedience, and so on. There is nothing romantic or heroic about sin in the Bible. Instead, its consequences are graphically depicted: judgment, death, disease, wars, broken families, unhappy lives.

If we stop and think about how the Bible portrays sin, we can understand why it is our great enemy. Sin is not just breaking a few rules; sin is an audacious attempt to put ourselves above God and everyone else. We are at war with reality; no wonder there are casualties on all sides. Regarding God, even believers wrestle with feeling alienated, resentful, suspicious, and indifferent. Regarding each other, the picture is equally bad. We are living in a world of sinners. Even a perfectly righteous man like Jesus suffered greatly in this life at our hands. Our greatest problems, however, are not the ones given us by other sinners but by ourselves.

It is easy—but wrong—to believe that all our problems are outside of us. If we could only change circumstances, if only other people would get their acts together, then life would be good. But I am firmly convinced that each of us is his or her *own* biggest problem. In this way, the experience of Jesus was markedly different from our own. Jesus' circumstances were not good—He suffered greatly at the hands of sinners—yet we see in His life a stability, a repose, an unshakable confidence. Even during His greatest suffering, His deep-rooted confidence in the Father never wavered. This broken world could not mar the inner man.

We sinners, on the other hand, make our own lives many times worse through our blind and self-centered responses to life. The enemies that drain the joy from our lives are fear, self-pity, resentment, irritability, wounded pride, and much more.

All of these things are rooted in sin, and all of them come from inside. No other human being could be as successful at causing us pain as we are at hurting ourselves. You can mistreat me, but you can't make me feel sorry for myself; you can't make me resent you; you can't fill my head with fantasies of retribution. Only I can do that. When we start to understand the terrible damage that sin is doing to our own peace of mind, we can see why an eternal life of righteousness is such a valuable promise.

When I think about the joy of being freed from my own sinfulness, my imagination often returns to a little story in Mark 6. Jesus and His disciples have been working hard, with no time even to eat. They are sobered by the news of John the Baptist's death. Jesus urges them to get in a boat with Him and go to a secluded spot, away from the crowds, so they can rest. But it is hard to hide in the middle of a lake. The crowds see where Jesus is going, and when the boat lands, the crowds are all there waiting. No rest, no seclusion—the grind starts all over again. Naturally, Jesus is terribly frustrated and gets back in the boat. . . .

Well, no. Actually, He does something quite different:

> And disembarking, He saw a great multitude, and He felt compassion for them because they were like sheep without a shepherd; and He began to teach them many things. (Mark 6:34)

We are not like Jesus. Would our first thought at a time of weariness and loss be compassion for those who stole our much-needed rest? But what a world it would be if we were! Our lives would be joyful, confident, stable, peaceful. Instead of constantly fighting our own humanity, we would be everything that a human being is supposed to be. Instead of the uphill battle to repair broken human relationships, our relationships would heal as automatically as our bodily cuts do now. This is what the world would be if the problem of sin were solved.

Chasing the Wind

Sin is not the only problem we face. The book of Ecclesiastes shows us that sin's curse is compounded by the death and futility that characterize life in this age. Solomon, after trying everything this world had to offer, found it ultimately unsatisfying. Not that it was all bad; it was just not *enough*. All such efforts to find fulfillment in this life he calls "chasing after the wind." We human beings desire something lasting and truly meaningful. In this age, however, death is the great thief who makes that impossible.

Some Christians may balk at using Ecclesiastes as a guide for their lives today. Isn't that all behind us now? Didn't Jesus come to give us abundant life? Isn't every day with Jesus sweeter than the day before? But although believers can and do experience profound joy, it is a joy in spite of our current circumstances, not because of them. Peter says we rejoice in spite of our trials because of the glory that awaits us when Jesus returns. And Paul agrees with Ecclesiastes about life in this age. He says God has purposely subjected the world to futility; the entire creation is groaning like a woman in labor, and believers are groaning along with it (Romans 8:18-25). The difference between Romans and Ecclesiastes, of course, is that Paul emphasizes the gospel as the answer to the futility of this age. Labor pains are only temporary and give way to the desired birth. God subjected the world to futility temporarily, "in hope that the creation itself also will be set free from its slavery to corruption into the freedom of the glory of the children of God" (Romans 8:20-21).

When Adam and Eve lost us our place in the garden, our circumstances went from very good to very bad. We all try to pretend that life now is "normal," that it never was and never could be any different—but deep down we know better. Life now is a lonely struggle for survival and meaning, a struggle which ultimately fails. We are cut off from our Creator, we scramble to keep body and soul together, we sometimes hurt and betray each other, and ultimately death robs our lives of any meaning we may have hoped for. This is the human story. Any salvation worth calling "salvation" must deal with the real human problems; that is, it must give back the fulfillment, meaning, joy, holiness — the life — that sin and death have stolen from us.

A Kingdom of Life

From Genesis on, God has announced in the Bible His intention to restore the world and save a people for Himself. He begins by promising Abraham that He will bless the entire world through Abraham. Revealing more and more of His intentions as time goes on, He tells Israel through the prophets that a new day is coming — for them and for the world. He will place a descendant of David on the throne of Israel, to rule not just Israel but all the nations of the earth. This anointed king, this "Messiah" or "Christ," will rule according to God's will and purpose. All hostility to God will cease, all enemies of God will fall, all sin will be cleansed from the world. God will remake the heavens and earth, and death will pass away. God will cleanse the hearts of His people. Over time, this blessed situation where God will rule through His chosen king came to be called "the kingdom of God."

The New Testament opens with the proclamation of "the gospel of the kingdom." The King has come, His kingdom is at hand, and when it is established there will be no sin and death. The gospel's promise of eternal life is not just a promise for an unending series of days like the one you had today. Rather, it is the promise of a life free from both the futility of death and the corrosive corruption of sin. All our relationships will be restored — our relationship with God, with each other, with creation, and with ourselves. The conquest of sin is absolutely central to what Jesus came to bring about in His kingdom:

> But according to His promise we are looking for new heavens and a new earth, in which righteousness dwells. (2 Peter 3:13)

> For we through the Spirit, by faith, are waiting for the hope of righteousness. (Galatians 5:5)

"But seek first His kingdom and His righteousness. . . . "
(Matthew 6:33)

The righteousness of the coming age makes it a desirable
place to be, which is why Jesus taught His disciples to pray:

"May your kingdom come,
May Your will be done on earth as it is in heaven."
(Matthew 6:10*)

If we understand the theology of the kingdom, this language
should be easy to understand. This present age ignores, violates,
and ridicules the moral will of God. The coming "kingdom" is
when God will establish His righteous rule on the earth. If we
understand how wonderful the conquest of sin will be, we will
long for that day with all our hearts. Jesus teaches us this in the
Lord's Prayer: In the deep expressions to God of our heart's
desire, the coming kingdom of righteousness should be one of
our highest priorities.

In the Beatitudes, Jesus describes those who hunger and
thirst for righteousness as "blessed." Jesus is not describing
the perfectly righteous; "hungering and thirsting" portrays a
pitiful lack—an empty stomach, a parched mouth, a longing
for what we do not have. Anyone who has ever thirsted understands the longing Jesus describes. What is the great hope of
those "who hunger and thirst after righteousness"? Jesus tells
us: "They shall be satisfied" (Matthew 5:6). After great thirst,
how satisfying that first deep drink is! The righteousness of
God's kingdom will satisfy the way a cool drink satisfies in the
desert. It will thrill the heart like the first day of freedom thrills
the lifelong slave. After all, we are slaves: "Every one who commits sin is the slave of sin. . . . If therefore the Son shall make
you free, you shall be free indeed" (John 8:34,36). The return
of Jesus as King is our liberation day, the day we escape the
prison of our own self-centeredness, finally enjoying God and
each other as we should.

WE MUST CHOOSE

The gospel, then, is the announcement of the solution to every-one's deepest problems, if only we knew it. However, the gospel is not speaking in a vacuum. Other competing voices have made their claims as well, more immediate claims of satis-faction and fulfillment. Believing the gospel means accepting its promises as true and rejecting the claims of all its com-petitors. Believing the gospel means choosing the kingdom of God over "the world."

As the saying goes, the Christian's enemies are "the world, the flesh, and the Devil." Why the Devil is our enemy is clear, why the flesh can trip us up is clear, but what is the problem with the world? Why is the Bible so concerned that we not be "worldly"? The obvious answer might seem to be that the world is an unrighteous place, and to be "worldly" is to follow the evil people of this world in their unrighteous ways. Not to be worldly, then, we need to keep ourselves free from a list of prohibited behaviors: drinking, fornication, gambling, and so on. Unfortu-nately, such a perspective has dangerously trivialized the prob-lem of worldliness.

This world is dangerous because it competes with the promises of God. In this world we learn how to take care of our-selves (we think) and supply what we "need": food and shelter; wealth and security against losing our wealth; other people to meet our emotional needs; something to do that gives our lives meaning; distracting pleasures. The list goes on and on. Expe-rience suggests these strategies work, and in the short term they often do, but something is fundamentally wrong with them: (1) They are only temporary; and (2) they do not address our real problems. Scripture makes clear that our real problems are the curse of sin and the futility of death, and the solutions *God* has provided are not temporary but eternal.

Therefore the true problem of worldliness is not solved by merely "keeping our act clean." We are worldly people if we have bought the lie that anything in this world can meet the deepest needs of our hearts. The world is in our face every day, while the kingdom of God seems remote and abstract. Never-theless, as we have seen, our true fulfillment is to be found in that kingdom. The world is dangerous because it can fatally dis-tract us from our own best interests; it can lead us to our eter-nal destruction by competing with the gospel.

> Do not love the world, nor the things in the world. If anyone loves the world, the love of the Father is not in him. For all that is in the world, the lust of the flesh and the lust of the eyes and the boastful pride of life, is not from the Father, but is from the world. And the world is passing away, and also its lusts; but the one who does the will of God abides forever. (1 John 2:15-17)

John had a firsthand opportunity to see the connection between faith and the prior commitments and desires of the heart. In his gospel, he tells various stories about people who accept or reject Jesus, and how their belief or unbelief is rooted in their desires. Those who don't follow Jesus want something different from what Jesus offers. We will look at two such stories.

How Can You Believe?

In John 5, a very dramatic and ironic scene shows us the great Jewish students of the law, those who pored over the scriptures day and night, staring right at the Messiah but refusing to believe. Jesus isn't surprised; in fact, He explains to them why they don't believe:

> "I have come in My Father's name, and you do not receive Me. . . . How can you believe, when you receive glory from one another, and you do not seek the glory that is from the one and only God?" (John 5:43-44)

What Jesus says here is profoundly important to anyone seeking to understand saving faith. Jesus' opponents are not able to believe because they have their hearts set on something dif-ferent from what God is offering. How can they believe when

Jesus is not playing the worldly "glory" game that means so much to them? To accept Jesus as the Christ means accepting Him for the particular kind of Christ He came here to be. Neither His life nor His teaching attracted them; their goals and His were incompatible.

Notice that Jesus does not scold His opponents for having desires but for having the wrong desires. To want glory is not a bad thing; Paul speaks approvingly of those who "by perseverance in doing good seek for glory and honor and immortality" (Romans 2:7). To want to be honored as significant and worthwhile is a natural human desire. But where and when do we expect that desire to be met? We can seek temporary glory today because the world approves of us, or we can seek eternal glory tomorrow because God approves of us. The glory which comes from men is immediate; it brings acclaim, security, wealth, self-satisfaction, and many other things in this world. The glory which comes from God brings few benefits in this world; however, it is the true glory, the honor truly worth having.

Jesus describes His opponents as those who don't believe in Him; He also describes them as those who want worldly rather than eternal glory. Ultimately these are two different ways of describing the same thing. They believe what they believe because they want what they want.

The Bread of Life
The great "bread of life" passage in John 6 provides another good example of how biblical faith in Jesus is connected to our true desires. A great crowd seeks Jesus the day after He miraculously fed five thousand people using five loaves and two fishes:

> Jesus answered them and said, "Truly, truly, I say to you, you seek Me, not because you saw signs, but because you ate of the loaves, and were filled. Do not work for the food which perishes, but for the food which endures to eternal life, which the Son of Man shall give to you, for on Him the Father, even God, has set His seal."
> (John 6:26-27)

The feeding of the five thousand was a miraculous sign that Jesus is the Messiah, the one sent by God. By this miracle, the Father was saying, "Yes, this truly is the promised Deliverer. Anyone who knows Me, anyone who longs for My promised salvation, should come to Him." Anyone coming to Jesus in this way, with this attitude, would then discover that He was not running for Messiah on a platform of "five loaves in every pot." Instead, Jesus came to provide the true need of every person: eternal life. And as we have seen above, eternal life is not just eternal breathing—it is a life eternally restored from the futility of death and the curse of sin.

Most of the hungry crowd, however, see only one thing: "This is a guy who can give us bread. Follow Him, and from this day forward the curse on the ground will be lifted; no more digging and hoeing and sweating." They made a profound mistake. Although the crowd is ready to "believe" in Jesus as the Messiah whom God sent, they do not agree with God about what they truly need. It is as if they learned the wrong lesson from the manna in the wilderness: Not "man lives by everything proceeding from the mouth of God," but rather, "man lives by bread, period; that's why God gave it to us." We can see this is exactly what the crowd thinks:

> They said therefore to Him, "What then do You do for a
> sign, that we may see, and believe You? What work do
> You perform? Our fathers ate the manna in the wilder-
> ness; as it is written, 'He gave them bread out of heaven
> to eat.'" (John 6:30-31)

The crowd's hint here is plain: "Isn't it clear, Jesus, what You need to do to win our trust? We know what we want from God. We want bread. God showed His willingness to bless us with bread when He gave the manna in the wilderness. Anyone who claims to be from God had better bless us in that same way again. Well, we're ready. Just lay some more of that miraculous bread on us, just like you did yesterday, and then we'll know that you are the right guy to follow."

The issue the crowd faces is fundamental. They will follow God (or anyone else) who will give them what they want, but they will not change their minds about what they truly need. They believe man lives by bread alone; if Jesus is prepared to agree to those terms, then they are prepared to follow Him.

Jesus, however, refuses to play along. He tells them His death on the cross, His flesh and His blood, are the only truly necessary "food." But the crowd is not looking for this, and many of them leave. Jesus asks His twelve disciples whether they want to leave as well, and in one of my favorite statements in the Bible, Peter answers, "Lord, to whom shall we go? You have words of eternal life" (John 6:68). However strange Jesus' language about "eating my flesh" might sound, Peter knows his need, wants what Jesus promised, and trusts Him to give it.

In one sense, all Jesus asks of the crowd is to believe in Him: "This is the work of God, that you believe in Him whom He has sent" (John 6:29). But to believe in Jesus requires a major revolution in the hearts of the people: They have to see their need for Jesus' death; and they have to want the eternal life He promises. None of these things is true of them. The crowd faces the same questions their forefathers faced in the wilderness: What do we really need? What do we really want? Whom do we really trust? They answer these questions wrongly, and so they leave.

In both John 5 and 6, Jesus explains the unbelief of His hearers in terms of their desires. Jesus is offering them an eternal solution to their deepest problems, but they are fatally distracted by things more immediate and temporary. Believing in Jesus requires each of us to face this choice. And the letters of the New Testament make it clear that this is not a one-time choice, but one that must be confirmed throughout our lives. Paul urges Timothy not to be seduced by worldly wealth but to "take hold of the eternal life to which you were called" (1 Timothy 6:12). James warns, "You adulteresses, do you not know that friendship with the world is hostility toward God?" (James 4:4). The gospel always confronts us with the choice: Do we want what the world offers, or do we want what God offers? The gospel cannot be an ornament tacked onto a worldly view of life; the gospel is an alternative to a worldly view of life.

CONCLUSION

In this chapter and the two preceding, I have tried to show the richness of the biblical concept of saving faith. The mere act of belief is not in itself significant; human beings can find all kinds of ungodly reasons to believe. The children of God have hearts made profoundly new; they believe because they are willing to see the hard truths about themselves, God, and the world:

- They see their need for the gospel because they know that they stand guilty and condemned.
- They see the reliability and importance of the gospel because they know and trust the God who gave it.
- They see the desirability of the gospel because they know that nothing in this world can compare with God's coming kingdom of righteousness.

At this point our friend Joe may be getting nervous. To Joe, this sounds an awful lot like other teachers who have troubled him in the past, the ones who say that Christians must make a "total commitment" at their conversion; otherwise, that conversion isn't genuine. This has always worried Joe. He became a Christian at summer camp, where he had gone because he had a crush on one of the counselors. On the last night of camp, a long, intimate talk with her about God left him dazzled and entranced (for several reasons). Around the campfire that night when the altar call came, he saw her looking at him expectantly. What else could he do but go forward? For several days, he was on a spiritual high, which he now suspects was nine-tenths hormones.

Joe has been wrestling with issues like "loving God" and "humility" and "not loving the world" ever since. The "humility" part he understands; he feels himself to be enough of a sinner that he couldn't deny it if he wanted to. But does he know, fear, and love God? Joe often prays for a greater love of God. He feels like such an unspiritual person at times. As for the world, Joe feels like he gets floored by every sucker punch the world throws him. Not that his life is constant defeat; sometimes he is strong in his resolve to follow God. Other times, however, the temptations come at him faster than he knows how to deal with them. He feels like he is stuck in quicksand—as fast as he can get one part of himself free of the world's clutches, another part is being sucked in. How do Joe's shaky conversion and inconsistent experience as a believer measure up to the grand picture of faith we have seen in these chapters?

Joe is right to recognize the seriousness of what I am saying. We are not necessarily saved just because we "believe" the story about Jesus. I want to assure Joe, however, that nothing in his life is inconsistent with the ideas presented so far. Believers do not necessarily understand or demonstrate all the right attitudes at once. These attitudes emerge over time, often through trials and suffering. This "sanctification" process is the primary means by which we come to know whether or not we have saving faith, and it continues throughout the lives of all true believers. We do not earn our salvation through the process, but it is God's way of showing us that we truly belong to Him, that we have a heart of faith. And we must be very clear: Having a heart of faith is not the same as being without sin. Joe's struggles with his own moral weaknesses do not call his faith into question.

Joe is right, I believe, to balk at the "total commitment" model of Christian conversion. In practice very few new believers have ever made such a commitment, nor would they even understand what such a commitment would mean. These are the lessons we learn over time. The Christian life is a combination of growth and struggle, sometimes the most growth emerging from the most struggle. If there is no growth, a serious question emerges whether there is any reality behind our "faith." But struggle and failure are only to be expected. Why does it work this way? What does the Bible say about this process? Joe should read on.

PART THREE

FAITH AT WORK

CHAPTER SIX

Faith Under Trial

⟍⟋

Enthusiasm leads many young Christians to stand on street corners, look strangers in the eye, and ask, "Are you saved?" In later years, after many discouraging failures, those same Christians may stand in front of the mirror, look themselves in the eye, and ask, "Are you saved?" Assurance of salvation is a troubling issue for many of us. Should our assurance be tied in any way to our behavior? When it comes to knowing our own standing before God, should we be in front of the mirror at all?

Assurance cannot begin with self-examination. Assurance must start with the character and promises of God. God is good, and He has promised to save people who are not good. The loving promise of God, not our performance, is the solid rock upon which all assurance must be built. However, a gospel of grace does not rule out self-examination altogether. As we have seen in previous chapters, a meaningful faith arises from a miraculous change of heart. Such a profound change cannot be hidden in the heart forever. If we truly have hearts for God, then our lives will show it. But this is neither easy nor immediate. The Bible gives a very specific description of how we come to understand our own hearts: *The true Christian perseveres under trial.*

THE PARABLE OF THE SOWER

The foundational teaching in the New Testament on perseverance comes from Jesus Himself, in the Parable of the Sower (Matthew 13, Mark 4, and Luke 8). In this parable, Jesus compares the gospel to a seed that needs the right kind of soil in which to grow. Jesus describes four different kinds of soil, each with an analogy to different states of the human heart.

First, some of the seed falls by the side of the road, on soil so hard-packed that the seed takes no root at all. This corresponds to those who hear the gospel and never respond.

Next, Jesus speaks of seed falling in soil so shallow and filled with rocks that the seed cannot send its roots very deep. When the sun arises, it scorches the weak, desiccated plant, and the plant dies. This corresponds to those who initially believe the gospel but who have no deep commitment to it. When the hard times come, their shallow belief disappears. The account in Luke 8 calls these hard times "times of testing." The Matthew account speaks more specifically of the times "when affliction or persecution arises because of the word." People who follow Jesus often find the world around them hostile to Christian faith; a belief that has not taken root in the heart will not survive such hostility.

After this, Jesus talks of the seed that falls in thorn-infested ground. The seed must compete with the thorns, and in the end the killer weeds choke out the young plant. In the same way, belief in the gospel will not survive in a heart already captured by the competition. Jesus describes this competition as "the worry of the world, and the deceitfulness of riches" (Matthew 13:22) and "the pleasures of this life" (Luke 8:14). For faith to come to its fruition, it must represent a choice of the kingdom of God over the kingdom of this world.

Finally, Jesus speaks of the seed falling in good ground, where it grows and provides the desired harvest. This corresponds to the heart of the true believer. Jesus describes such ones as those "who have heard the word in an honest and good heart, and hold it fast, and bear fruit with perseverance" (Luke

8:15). Because their hearts are receptive, their response is one of tenacious, life-changing belief. They believe deeply, permanently, and to great effect.

Some argue that the parable of the sower does not teach that believers must endure. Rather, salvation is an issue only for the first group, those represented by the seed beside the road, and the issue for the other three is not salvation, but "bearing fruit." "Bearing fruit" is variously interpreted: Some would say it means to make converts; others would say it means to grow in godliness. Either way, "bearing fruit" is a separate issue from salvation.

I have two responses:

1. This interpretation does not make sense of the analogy Jesus is making. Any farmer knows that the sower is interested in only one thing: the harvest. The "fruit" in the parable stands for everything that results when a true heart (the soil) responds to the gospel (the seed). On the right kind of heart, the gospel has a profound effect; on the wrong kind, nothing of significance results. The analogy makes no sense otherwise. Whether the plant never grows, or withers in the sun, or is choked out and fruitless, it is all the same in the end; a farmer counts all three cases as total failures. The power of the analogy is derived from experience. "Think," Jesus is saying, "of the different kinds of soil that in the end produce nothing; it is the same with the human heart."

2. Why would we suppose this parable is not about salvation? When we look at the larger context of the New Testament, we find exactly the same idea expressed—salvation comes to those who persevere despite persecution and the temptations of the world.

In the parable of the sower, Jesus vividly pictures three ways in which the gospel can fail to have the desired effect in someone's life: (1) One can refuse to believe from the beginning; (2) One can have a weak commitment that cannot survive hostility and persecution; and (3) One can have divided and competing loyalties, where worldly interests choke out initial interest in the gospel. Only one response results in salvation—a response out of "an honest and good heart." Such a heart is not hard; it is not shallow; it is not divided. Because the heart is not hard, it responds to the gospel with belief. Because the heart is not shallow, belief puts down deep roots and can survive the opposition of the world. Because the heart is not divided, belief is not nullified by stronger loves and loyalties. The heart of the believer is fertile ground for the gospel, and thus belief will and must persevere.

Being a man who has struggled with many weaknesses in my own life, I want to say something about the "undivided" heart of the believer. Jesus is not suggesting that there is no struggle. We all wrestle in this life with what our ultimate loyalties and desires are. We are not so pure that we never falter along the way. But which side wins? In His analogy, the thorns choke out the budding plant. Jesus is talking about the bottom line: In the end, have the promises of God or "the pleasures of this life" captured my heart?

THE PROVING OF YOUR FAITH

Granted that perseverance is necessary for salvation, what does this have to do with assurance of salvation? In Romans 5, Paul articulates the surprising connection between perseverance and assurance:

> And not only this, but we also boast in our tribulations, knowing that tribulation brings about perseverance; and perseverance, proof; and proof, hope. . . . (Romans 5:3-4*)

The first chapters of both James and 1 Peter echo Paul's thought.

> Consider it all joy, my brethren, when you encounter various trials, knowing that the proving of your faith

produces perseverance. Blessed is a man who perseveres under trial; for once he has been approved, he will receive the crown of life, which He has promised to those who love Him. (James 1:2-3, 12*)

In this you greatly rejoice, even though now for a little while, if necessary, you have been distressed by various trials, that the proof of your faith, being more precious than gold which is perishable, even though tested by fire, may be found to result in praise and glory and honor at the revelation of Jesus Christ. (1 Peter 1:6-7*)

Contained in these three passages is a progression of ideas—from tribulation to perseverance to proof to hope—essential to understanding the biblical notion of assurance; in fact, it is essential to understanding what God is doing in our lives as believers.

We boast in our tribulations. . . . Amazingly, Paul, James, and Peter all see trials and tribulations as something *desirable*. James and Peter say trials are something in which to rejoice. Paul says we "boast in our tribulations." Ironically, as Paul makes clear earlier in Romans, tribulations are almost the only things we have in which to boast since we can't boast in our works. We can boast in our troubles, however, because they are ultimately a sign of God's favor.

Why does Paul say this? And why do James and Peter also say trials are something in which to delight? The answer is central to our topic: Troubles are desirable because ultimately they result in the very assurance of salvation for which we long.

If "tribulations" (troubles) are such desirable things, we had better start by determining what a "tribulation" is. We all know what we mean when we talk about troubles—the things that aggravate us, that annoy us, that cause us suffering and pain. But not every difficulty counts as "trouble" in Paul's sense. James and Peter are more specific in their description. They talk about "trials" and "the proving of our faith." Peter compares the testing of our faith with the testing of gold in the fire. In a trial, some question is being examined. Is there real gold in this lump of rock? Is this bridge strong enough to hold me? In Christian trials, the question is this: Are we people of saving faith? God knows, but we don't. Trials and tribulations help us to find out.

When we first become believers, we only dimly understand the implications of the gospel. In this present age, God's kingdom is intangible and mostly invisible, while the world is with us every minute. Yes, we say we believe the gospel, but who knows how real that "belief" is? When our faith is tested, we find out. It is one thing to say, "I believe," when nothing tangible is at stake. A trial is like a splash of cold water—it wakes us up; it forces us to choose. Trials force us to trust the God we can't see, in the middle of a world we can see.

Knowing that tribulation brings about perseverance. . . . As we saw in the parable of the sower, the one who perseveres in faith to the end will be saved. But the passages in Romans, James, and 1 Peter say more—they say perseverance plays some part in assuring us of our own salvation now.

This may seem puzzling at first. The need to persevere can sound quite daunting. If we have to endure to the end, how can we know before the end whether we are saved? It sounds like a deadly game of musical chairs: It doesn't matter whether you have a chair now; it only matters if you are sitting at the end.

In fact, many argue for assurance precisely by *denying* the need for perseverance. They say, "You can be assured you are saved because it doesn't matter whether you persevere in faith or not." That sounds like a kind and simple solution, but it is unnecessary and misguided. Perseverance rightly understood is compatible with assurance; in fact, assurance and perseverance are very tightly linked.

Perseverance is only scary if we think about it as a race we must run on our own. If the message is, "It's up to you to endure to the end," then all we can say now is, "Well, I haven't given up yet." But what might we do tomorrow? What if we work hard and almost get there and then run out of gas right at the end? Well, that's tough; only those who make it to the end will be saved. Perhaps we should hope to die young, before we have a chance to change our minds.

However, perseverance is more than just crossing a finish line some day in the future. Perseverance is a quality built into the believing heart itself and so shows itself today, in this life. At certain points in our lives God brings us to a fork in the road. Will we keep going down the gospel path? Or is something else—maybe money or freedom from suffering or popularity— more important? The decision to persevere when something real is at stake says something now: it provides what the Bible calls "proof."

And perseverance, proof. . . . Perseverance provides "proof" or "approvedness"—the end product, the result—of going through trials. A trial takes a certain question, tests it, and the result is proof; one knows the answer after the test. Paul, James, and Peter say that perseverance in trials provides proof *now* that we are people of faith.

When we first say, "I believe," our faith is essentially invisible. People "get religion" for many reasons, but those reasons are not immediately apparent. Trials provide the background against which our invisible faith can start to show itself. Something that floats downstream may blend so well with the water that it is invisible; when it swims upstream, however, resisting the water's pressure, it leaves a wake everyone can see. Perseverance is the wake my faith leaves as it swims upstream through the world.

And proof, hope. . . . Paul's chain of logic in Romans 5:3-4 starts with "troubles" (tribulations) and ends with "hope." Hope is the desirable outcome; hope is what makes troubles something to boast in.

Our hope, as the Bible describes it, is not merely wishful thinking, as in "I hope it doesn't snow." Hope, in the biblical sense, is a confident desire. When we hope for something, we *want* it and we *expect* it. God has promised us that one day sin and death will lose their corrosive grip on human life; this is our hope, our confident desire. Having our faith "proven" through trials increases our confidence that we will receive what we long for. In other words, to grow in hope is to grow in assurance of our salvation.

And hope does not disappoint. .... Ultimately, however, our hope is only meaningful if the one we have trusted is reliable. Paul concludes his discussion of tribulations in Romans 5 by reminding us that our hope will not disappoint us; what we have hoped for will happen because it is God who is committed to making it happen. Our trials teach us we are believers, and the great news is that God is unchangeably committed to believers. The foundation of our assurance is not our own faith, but God's love.

Trials don't teach us to say, "Wow, look at how much faith I've got!" Rather, trials inspire an assurance with a major and a minor theme: The major theme tells of God's unshakable love; the minor theme tells of the reality of our own trust in that love. Trials teach us to say, "God alone is worthy of my love and trust; I rejoice to *see* that I am learning to trust Him." Having seen this, our hope—our assurance—will be deeply strengthened.

CLARIFYING SOME ISSUES

Misunderstandings can arise over what exactly "trials" are all about, so a few explanations are in order.

We are not masochists. Christians don't welcome trials for their own sake; nobody enjoys suffering. Exhortations, such as "rejoice in trials," are not intended to make people feel guilty when they feel the pain of suffering; troubles are as difficult for Christians as for anyone else. These passages are not saying pain is not painful to Christians. They are saying, however, that trials can be important because they tell us something about ourselves we really want to know.

We are not proving our moral perfection. Trials are not intended to prove our goodness and freedom from sin. We are not proving we are morally perfect; we are proving we have faith. If I snap impatiently at my wife, the situation certainly "tests" something about me: It tests my character, the presence or absence of evil in me; it shows my selfishness, self-pity, or impatience. But it does not necessarily test my *faith*; if it did, none of us could pass such a test. A trial in the biblical sense tests our commitment to the truths of God, not our moral perfection.

We may—in fact, we probably will—make many foolish and sinful choices in the midst of trials. Trials are difficult. We struggle. We flounder. We take the wrong road and then come back. But the issue is not whether we are good enough to keep from falling into sin; we all sin. The issue is whether at the end we still want God's kingdom. The proof we seek is whether we trust God enough and love Him enough to continue on with Him.

We are not being asked to prove ourselves. These passages are not telling us to go out and *do something* to prove we are believers; in terms of the arguments they present, that would be impossible. We cannot provide our own trials and tribulations; the students don't know enough to be able to write their own midterm exam. Assurance is a gift from God, a gift that requires much suffering to unwrap. No timetable is presented; no promises of when and where are given. We are only told, when the troubles come to test our faith, that we should welcome and rejoice in them because God is showing us something truly important about ourselves.

The test is not for God's sake, but for ours. The point of perseverance is growth in self-knowledge. God already knows me, seeing straight into my heart without any need for the external evidence of my life. If I die immediately after I turn to Christ in faith, am I disqualified because I didn't go through testing? No! If I die while I am in the middle of a crisis of faith, am I disqualified from salvation? No! My salvation depends on the true state of my heart, which God alone knows. Testing and perseverance are a merciful gift of God, intended for me today, in this life. Through them I come to know myself as a believer.

"Assurance" is only an issue for us while we live in this world. The man who converts on his deathbed has no need to prove his faith through trials; he is about to find the answers to all his questions. His friends who remain behind cannot have perfect assurance of his destiny, but when did God ever promise us that He would tell us another's story?

Mere longevity is not enough. Mere longevity of belief does not prove that someone is a true child of God. Many hardhearted legalists have persevered in their self-righteous religion right to the end. God uses the combination of *trials* and perseverance to give His children the proof they seek. Trials force the issue. Trials give us immediate, experiential knowledge of God. We learn God means serious business; He runs a very hard school. In trials we learn that God will willingly sacrifice our present comfort and happiness to save us from sin and death. Only those who trust God and want what He offers will stay for such treatment. Each trial makes the cost of discipleship more clear to us. The fact that we continue to persevere is the surest proof that the miracle of faith is at work in our hearts.

THE TRIALS AND TRIBULATIONS OF JOE

We set out in this book to answer Joe's questions about his struggles as a Christian. He is already in a good position to understand about trials. Joe has seen this very process at work in his own life.

Soon after Joe became a Christian, he became part of the lay leadership in his church. He decided, "My goal in life is to go to seminary, become a pastor, and find a good Christian woman to marry." He prayed, "God, I want to be in your service. Show me which seminary I should go to, help me find the woman I should marry, and help me get over the obstacles in my way, so that I can serve You."

God responded to this prayer by sending Joe a series of setbacks; at least, they were setbacks from Joe's perspective. First of all, he met a woman who seemed ideal—she was a good Christian and even played the organ. Naturally, Joe asked her to marry him. But nine months after they married, they had kids they were not expecting. In fact, they had triplets—hyperactive triplets. Joe and his wife now spent most of their time tired and discouraged, trying to keep up with the never-ending demands from their kids. His wife started to change; she soon sickened of the nominal Christianity of her childhood and abandoned the faith.

Joe discovered that although he was bright, he was not a very good worker; he was undisciplined and not a self-starter. He found it hard to keep jobs, and he never made even close to enough money for seminary. By this time there was real stress in the marriage, and eventually Joe's wife took off with a younger and richer man, leaving Joe with the children.

Joe didn't know it, but he was in the middle of the major trial of his life. God was opening for Joe a window on his own heart. Until this time of terrible difficulty, Joe would have been hard-pressed to explain his own life. Did he become a Christian out of faith or only out of a desire for religious respectability? Did he want to go to seminary to learn about God or only to prove he was smart and worthy of respect? Did he want to be a pastor to serve or only to gain power and prestige? Joe's heart, like everyone's, is deceitfully wicked; who knows what he was really thinking? Joe was about to find out.

It took a long time. Joe's initial response was to be impatient with his children, embittered toward his ex-wife, and envious of his successful friends. He was especially tempted to be furious with God. He was horrified by these feelings, but he succumbed to them often. This is not surprising. Trials would not be trials if they were easy. Over time and with much struggle, Joe came very close to telling God to get lost—but Joe never did.

One event was particularly important in Joe's journey of discovery. After the divorce, Joe started hanging around with some of his old nonChristian buddies, who took him one night to a sleazy bar downtown. (The triplets were with Grandma.) Not being used to alcohol, Joe got drunk and ended up going to bed with a woman he met in the bar. The horror he felt the next day shook Joe to the bottom of his soul. He started to realize how self-righteous he was. He had always prided himself on his moral behavior, and he was shocked to learn that he was capable of such gross immorality. He couldn't lie to himself anymore; he was not the good little Christian boy he liked to consider himself. He was a *sinner*. Never before in his life had the cross of Christ made so much sense to him. The cross is about forgiveness and restoration, and Joe began to realize how much he needed both.

At this point in Joe's life the thinking began in earnest. God had never promised Joe a big ministry; He promised to give Him eternal life. Was that enough for Joe? Trials forced Joe to think seriously for the first time about his own evil heart, about God's incredible kindness in sending Jesus to die for him, and about the precious promise that one day all the crud in his selfish little soul will be cleaned out. Oh, he would have said that he understood all that before; he had even taught a Sunday school class about "Salvation for Sinners." Now, however, Joe was having his own personal encounter with the truth of these ideas. Joe came to the amazing conclusion that he wanted what God has promised in the gospel, even if God never gives him a prestigious ministry or a great marriage or anything else he always felt to be essential to happiness. God took a tempting and distracting piece of the world and said, "Joe, I know you want this, but you can't have it." Because of this, Joe learned something about God's priorities in a forceful and tangible way. He also learned something about his own priorities; Joe trusted God even after God had dashed most of Joe's worldly hopes. (In the end, God was kind to Joe in another way; his ex-wife went through a spiritual shaking of her own and returned to God and Joe.)

The heart of the believer is humble, trusting, and hungry for what God has promised; those real qualities in Joe's heart kept him committed to God through all his troubles. In his heart a major battle was fought between the kingdom of this world and the kingdom of God—and God won.

This is the model of trials and how they lead to assurance. We can't really know whether we have put our trust in God until something is at stake, until something grabs us by the throat and reminds us that God and the world are really going in two different directions. As long as they seem to be going in the same direction, we can't know whether we are following God or following the world. Only as they part company do we realize we have to make a choice. When the boat is tied up, it's easy to stand with one foot on the boat and one foot on the dock. God occasionally does His children the great kindness of starting the boat and pulling away from the dock. They may get wet for a while, but eventually God's children will discover themselves in the boat with Him, and then they will rejoice.

ALTERNATIVE MODELS OF ASSURANCE

Many people have argued that Christians can have assurance of salvation, but they would not agree with the picture I have just painted. The disagreement usually concerns the role that self-examination plays in assurance. Let's examine briefly three other commonly presented models.

Assurance and the Stake Behind the Barn

I was first taught the "stake behind the barn" model of assurance. This model invites us to go out behind the barn in our imagination and plant a stake in the ground; on the stake we write "On November 19, 1971 (or whenever) I accepted Jesus as my Savior." If we ever doubt our salvation, we can look at the stake behind the barn. To look at any other aspect of our life and behavior would be wrong.

Three beliefs support this model: (1) Faith is simple and obvious—we could not be mistaken about whether we have saving faith; (2) faith has no necessary connection with how we live; and (3) faith is a one-time event; perseverance is not necessary. (Not everyone who might use the "stake behind the barn" language would agree to all these points. But many would, and this is certainly how I was taught it.) This perspective seems to be a have-your-cake-and-eat-it-too brand of Arminianism. In classic Arminianism, which emphasizes the independent free will of human beings, anyone can lose their salvation by simply choosing to stop believing. The "stake-behind-the-barn" model of assurance is semi-Arminian; we can have an independent free will *and* assurance because nothing we go on to choose can affect our salvation. One simple act of belief tells us we got in the door, and nothing we do can get us kicked out again.

This perspective is misguided. It tries to take the sting out of the idea of perseverance, but it has done it in the wrong way. All three of the supporting tenets of this perspective are wrong. First, faith is not simple and obvious; it arises out of a radical change of perspective about God, myself, and the world. In this life, only time can show whether the words "I believe" are truly rooted in this change of heart. Second, saving faith does change how we live. I will argue in another chapter that this is what James means in his "faith without works" passage. Third, faith is not a one-time event, but a permanent change of heart which, if given time, will show itself in perseverance.

Assurance and the Knowledge of God's Love

A second model argues that faith is the knowledge that God loves us and is saving us. To have faith is to have God-given knowledge of our personal salvation. When faith is operating as it should be, assurance comes automatically. Therefore it is wrong to seek assurance by looking at our own behavior in any way because that is turning our eyes in the wrong direction. Our attention should be turned toward Christ, the One who has saved us.

This model is right in a way. Faith does involve a growing confidence that God will keep His promises to us personally. And our attention should be on the love of God, not on our own performance. We saw in Romans 5 that Paul ultimately appeals to the loving character of God; our hope will not fail because God is committed to His children. And this perspective rightly warns us against trying to "prove" we are saved by "doing something for God." It rightly warns us that our own works are not righteous enough to bring us assurance of God's favor. At any point of fear and doubt in our own lives, it is always right to turn our eyes from our own failures and look instead at God's loving promise to forgive and to restore us.

This model, however, wrongly tells us that we should not look at ourselves at all when seeking assurance of salvation. God intends trials to teach us something about ourselves as well as about Himself. Trials clear the fog from the eyes of God's people, and this gives us two kinds of knowledge: (1) We see the cross of Christ and the kingdom of God more clearly, and God and His promises rightly become the focus of our attention; but also (2) we see the change in ourselves. A blind man who gains his sight spends most of his time looking out at the new world; this is true. Surely, however, he spares a thought or two for himself, rejoicing that he is not blind anymore.

Assurance and Moral Success

A third model argues that saving faith must involve a certain level of obedience and moral success. This is what many understand lordship salvationists to be saying. We cannot be assured we are saved unless we have turned from sin and submitted ourselves to Christ in total obedience. Perseverance is required, yes—a perseverance in righteousness. As Christians, we should see the moral direction of our lives getting better and better; if we don't, then we are not truly Christians at all. Is this, in fact, what lordship salvationists mean? I don't know. Since many readers, however, have gotten the impression that lordship salvationists mean exactly this, it is worth responding to.

There is an element of truth in this model. Saving faith unquestionably makes a difference in the moral direction of our lives. Faith opens our eyes to our own sinfulness; faith gives us a gnawing hunger for the righteousness we still lack. And as I will argue in the next several chapters, saving faith does make a difference in the way we live. Our entire worldview has changed; of course our actions will change with it.

But with language like "total submission" and "obedience," questions inevitably arise. How do we reconcile concepts like "total surrender" with the reality of sin in every believer's life? Believers do sin. We often struggle with desires that are selfish, lustful, envious, greedy, and on and on. Sometimes, especially in the midst of great trials, we give in to those desires in ugly ways. Unless we carefully explain what we mean by "perseverance in righteousness," we end up making assurance virtually impossible. Every moral failure must cause us to doubt whether we are really saved. Only those who have gotten their moral act together can feel any confidence, and that confidence will go right out the window if they ever slip.

The biblical picture of assurance is very different. Saving faith does not guarantee moral victory today, or even tomorrow. It is, however, a permanent reorientation of our hearts to the evil in the world and in ourselves. We are growing to love God and hate evil, including the evil we still see in ourselves. In a way, the fact that sometimes we feel like we're getting worse instead of better is more evidence of the change God has brought about. Instead of hiding from our sin and trying to justify it, we are growing more willing to see how deep our moral problem really runs. Instead of the glib promises of our youth that we are "totally sold out to God," in our maturity we grow much more distrustful of ourselves. We have learned to recognize sin in its respectable disguises; we know now that only a miracle will ever disentangle us from the grip of our own selfishness.

Trials teach us that we truly do trust God to solve our problem, even if at times we feel as far from the goal as ever. Not the absence of sin, but the presence of persevering faith assures us that we are believers. Imagine a man who commits the same sin hundreds of times and each time comes back to God, saying, "Father, I know you love me; save me from this evil." It is still possible for this man to have every confidence that he will be saved; in fact, he may have more right to be assured than many others who are proud that they have never committed that sin at all.

CONCLUSION

In the next several chapters, we will talk about the next step, the relationship between a persevering faith and a change in our moral behavior. But what we have looked at in this chapter tells us that perseverance in faith itself is perhaps *the* crucial sign that true faith is present. This picture makes sense to me. I have seen God do this very thing in the lives of Christians I know; it has been true in my own life. I have become convinced that the testing of our faith, and the assurance that results from it, is one of the central features of the Christian experience.

We started out asking whether the one who seeks assurance of salvation has any business standing in front of the mirror. Basically, my answer is no. The mirror implies a kind of scrutiny and rigorous self-examination that cannot fail to discourage us. At this stage of our journey, our hearts are such a mixture of faithfulness and evil, truth and error, that none of us can stand up to such an examination. When doubts about our salvation assail us, the mirror is the last place to look. But it would be very right, every now and again, to look in our scrapbooks. The scrapbook shows the trials we have faced and the direction our lives have taken over time. On this page is the napkin from the restaurant where Fred's girlfriend jilted him for "getting so religious." Here is the doctor's report that told Sally she will never have children. On this page is the brochure with the picture of the big house that Tom could never afford after his illness. These pages tell the story of painful and precious lessons learned; they commemorate the battlefields where faith went to war. Fred and Sally and Tom were bruised and bloodied, but their faith proved itself to be real and tenacious; such proof was worth all the battle scars.

If the greatest thing God ever did for us was to send Jesus to the cross, then perhaps the second greatest thing He has done is to give us our troubles. Troubles ultimately assure us that our hearts have been remade by our Creator, that we are bound for a glorious destination, well worth every difficult minute of the journey.

CHAPTER SEVEN

The Wisdom from Above

If God had asked me, I would have urged Him to give me my glorious eternal inheritance immediately when I first became a believer. He didn't ask me. In fact, I soon discovered, as most Christians do, that the Christian life is hard. We live in a hostile environment, and we are here for the duration. Life does have its satisfactions, but they cannot protect us from the heartaches that the world gives us—or the heartaches that we give ourselves.

We are like the children of Israel on their way through the wilderness to the Promised Land; we are now citizens of a great kingdom, but we still have a long, sometimes weary journey home.

Clearly God knows what our struggles and burdens are in this life, and just as clearly He does not intend to relieve us of them immediately. He obviously sees value in our troubles, a value that is sometimes invisible to us. Trials bring wisdom, and God's unchangeable purpose for His children, which is the focus of His activity in the present age, is to make us wise. Why would I say this? What is so important about wisdom? What does this have to do with the question of who is saved and who isn't? These are the questions we will consider in this chapter.

In Defense of Wisdom

For as long as we are in this life, the pursuit of wisdom is a non-negotiable, life-and-death matter; by the end of the chapter I hope to have made clear why I say that. It may seem surprising, however, to claim so much for a quality we sometimes value so little. For some, the word "wisdom" conjures up pictures of bearded sages sitting on mountaintops, or pipe-smoking professors of philosophy. Such pictures suggest wisdom is an elite, esoteric pursuit, far removed from the practical matters of life. Others admire wisdom very much — in someone else. In daily life, however, the personal price for obtaining wisdom can seem too high; wisdom often seems to come through loss and suffering. For whatever reasons, people tend to push wisdom toward the bottom on their list of priorities. This is terribly short-sighted. As we will see, wisdom is a staple of life — like water and food, like air.

Understanding the Most Important Things

Biblical wisdom is hard to describe simply. Whatever word we might use to describe it always needs to be qualified; it is always "X, but more than X." For instance:

- Wisdom has an element of knowledge, but it is more than knowledge. Fools can gain knowledge and remain fools; the technological advances of the twentieth century prove that. However, one cannot be wise without knowing things.
- Wisdom has an element of practical experience, but it is more than experience. Fools can have numerous experiences and remain fools. However, one of the qualities of wisdom is its connection with reality. The wise one will have enough experience to know the way things really are.
- Wisdom has an element of personal integrity, but it is more than integrity. Fools can be honestly and sincerely foolish. However, wisdom always involves a

personal willingness to profit from knowledge and experience, even at great personal cost. Wisdom demands qualities like honesty, humility, courage, and perseverance; otherwise life's lessons must go unlearned.

So here is my attempt to define wisdom: *Wisdom is a skill at living life, derived from knowledge, experience, and the integrity to follow where they lead.* The wise person knows how to deal successfully with some portion of reality. There is a road to be traveled, a goal to be reached, and the wise person has the knowledge, experience, and desire to make it. We say of the wise person, "She's savvy, he's been down this road before, he's experienced, she has great maturity, he's got what it takes."

A wise person, however, is not equally understanding in all areas. Wisdom comes in many varieties, depending on what area of life is under discussion. For instance, the apostle Paul compares himself to a "wise master builder." Such a builder understands what it takes to make a successful building. For example, experience tells him what will happen if the foundation is built of shoddy materials. A novice builder will not know what to do or why. Likewise, a wise mother knows from experience what will push her child over the edge. A wise doctor knows from experience the signs of health and the signs of sickness. In any area of life, true wisdom comes from being in touch with some piece of reality. If through experience we have a feel for what is real, and if we are determined to act on what we know, then we are wise in some sense.

Not all wisdom, however, is created equal. The most profound wisdom looks at the whole picture and puts first things first. To understand a piece of reality is not enough; we want to understand the part of reality that is going to have the biggest effect on us. True wisdom requires a large enough frame of reference.

An analogy will show what I mean. Tom, Dick, and Harry are all at the same party. Tom watches a young man nervously moving about the room, trying to meet young women. Tom smiles at the young man's clumsy attempts; he says to himself, "Watch a master at work." Tom is an experienced party-animal; he knows exactly what to say and what not to say. In no time at all, Tom is the life of the party.

Meanwhile, Dick is watching Tom, thinking about how shortsighted Tom is. Tom can waste his time partying if he wants to; Dick has more important things to attend to. Dick has developed an unerring instinct for finding every wealthy, successful person in the room; he knows just what to say to make them remember him when they are trying to fill some important job. Tom can party his brains out if he wants; tomorrow Tom will have a hangover, and Dick will have a secure financial future.

Meanwhile, Harry is watching Tom and Dick, thinking about how shortsighted they both are. Although they are savvy guys, Harry thinks they have both been wasting their time. Harry alone has remembered this party is being held in a stateroom on the Titanic, and he is busy memorizing the locations of all the lifeboats. Harry is a social dunce and his job prospects are dim; however, he is the only one of them who knows how to get off a sinking ship.

Who is wisest? In one sense, each is wise in his own way; each has the necessary savvy and determination to be successful in his goals. Clearly, however, Harry has the broadest frame of reference; Harry's wisdom is the most significant. Harry is going to survive when Tom and Dick perish. To be truly wise, one doesn't have to understand everything, just the most important things.

Worldly Wisdom

We can understand, therefore, why the Bible looks down on "worldly wisdom." Within its own boundaries, the wisdom of the world can be true and workable; however, its boundaries are fatally limited. The Christian gospel is the ultimate wisdom because it alone has taken into account the eternal, spiritual realities. A "worldly" perspective is worldly precisely because it limits its vision to this world; something is wise if it pays off in this world, right now. But by narrowing its vision to the here and now, the world has missed the fundamental truth of existence: God Himself. Life goes on day by day, and people can become very skillful, very savvy, in dealing with the stuff in front of their face. But they don't want to know anything more, and so they don't. They know every inch of the Titanic's lovely inner rooms but will not look out over the bow: "No sir, there are no icebergs in these waters. And anyway, this ship is unsinkable, right?"

Paul warns of this problem in his letter to the Corinthians, a people quite capable of being seduced by the wisdom of the world, especially if it sounded eloquent and profound. Some of them were embarrassed by Paul's gospel; compared to other more flashy rhetoric, Paul's style and message sounded, well, foolish. Paul minces no words with them:

Where is the wise man? Where is the scribe? Where is the debater of this age? Has not God made foolish the wisdom of the world? For since in the wisdom of God the world through its wisdom did not come to know God, God was well-pleased through the foolishness of the message preached to save those who believe.
(1 Corinthians 1:20-21)

Paul's ultimate indictment of worldly wisdom is this: Through it one does not come to know God. The "wise" man of this age thinks he understands life very well, and given his limited perspective, he does. The wisdom of this age makes sense—if there were no God, if humanity were not under God's wrath, if each person did not face the choice of eternal life or eternal condemnation. Once we see that our eternal destiny is at stake, however, the world's wisdom shows itself for the short-sighted folly it is. A wisdom that misses the most important truths is not true wisdom.

The Bible is clear: In order to be wise, we must deal rightly with the most important realities. But the most important realities are doubly invisible to us—invisible because spiritual truths are difficult to see at the best of times; invisible again because we tend to resist spiritual truths anyway. But these are the truths we must confront; these are the icebergs upon which our snug little lives are going to founder and break. From the Bible's perspective, wisdom is a matter of life and death.

WISDOM AND TRIALS

Now I suspect that most Christians would agree with everything I have said—up to a point. If we focus only on a person's initial conversion, then certainly we can agree that wisdom is a life and death matter. When the gospel first confronts us, we must make the "wise" choice: We must choose truth over lies, life over death, belief over unbelief. Every believer has made a truly wise decision; every unbeliever is a fool.

The debate is over what happens in the rest of a Christian's life. If we do not, in some manner, demonstrate the reality of God-given wisdom, does this call into question our salvation? The answer is "yes," but I have some explaining to do before this answer makes sense.

To start, consider the analogy of a man's marriage vows. He stands before his friends and family, pledging to be faithful to his wife, promising to stay with her whatever comes, for better or for worse. Most men probably mean it when they say it, as far as it goes. But that is the question: How far does it go? Is this promise rooted in the personal integrity of the groom, a commitment to his bride and to the values of loyalty and loving sacrifice? Or is it just an expedient thing to say to get a woman to live with him? These questions can't be answered on the wedding day. With our limited human vision, a man's heart is a puzzle that only time can solve. One day a more attractive woman may come along; one day the wife's faults may have become clear to him (as his have become to her). When he leaves, looking for greener pastures, we see his more informed choice, his real values. When he said "for better or for worse," he hadn't really experienced what that would mean. When experience opened his eyes, he changed his mind. Likewise, a husband who stays has also made a more informed choice. Now that he knows something of what "for worse" means, he renews his intention to remain faithful knowledgeably. He doesn't just talk loyalty; he is loyal.

We should not take this analogy too far; we do not go in and out of salvation, being justified and then becoming unjustified again. But from our perspective in this life, salvation is very much like this marriage analogy. Some who make an initial profession of faith have a heart for God; others do not. For as long as we are in this world, our lives are all about confirming and reconfirming our choice to trust God. Growth in Christian wisdom is not so much about learning new lessons and new ideas; it is learning the old lessons again more deeply, learning in practice what we believe in theory. If time shows that we will not learn those lessons, then the question arises whether those beliefs were ever more than theory to us.

I want to be as clear as possible in what I am saying and not saying. The Bible does not teach that anyone has to qualify for salvation by demonstrating a certain amount of wisdom. The "thief on the cross" exception always holds. If we die young, or if we are slow learners, we have not disqualified ourselves from salvation by failing to earn enough brownie points. God alone sees the inner person; He doesn't need the evidence of later life choices to know a person's heart. *But we do.* We cannot have confidence that we are children of God if the essential stance of our life is rebellion and hostility to the truth.

At this point the idea of "trials of faith" becomes crucial once again. As we saw in the last chapter, the Bible argues that trials and tribulations are ultimately desirable because they help us to see the reality of our own faith. In the process of persevering through trials, however, we cannot help but grow wiser in the process. Perseverance and wisdom are two sides of the same coin. Perseverance means "staying the course even when the going gets rough." Why do we stay? We stay because we have wrestled with some aspect of the gospel and found it compelling. We saw that in Joe's life. During Joe's years of trial, when neither his marriage nor his ministry came out the way he wanted, Joe became wiser. Joe had not realized it, but his plans had been based largely on a lust for financial success and religious respectability. When God withheld these things, Joe had to ask himself whether the real promises of the gospel were enough for him. God promised forgiveness and the hope of eternal life, a life freed from the dark curse on this world. Joe had always known this in theory, but now he had to decide what God's promises really meant to him, whether they were actually more valuable than what he had lost in this world. When Joe finally said, "I trust you, Lord, no matter what," he knew what he was saying in a way he never had before. The kingdom of God had become more real to his mind and heart, as tangible as the money and prestige he had lost. Joe will go through other trials in his life, but never again will the world be as successful at fooling him; his sufferings have made him wise. He will recognize that the new trial is just the same choice in a new disguise; the same wolf is wearing a new sheep's clothing.

In order to embrace the implications of our faith, we must let go of deeply held—but wrong—convictions about life. This is a painful process, and by ourselves we would probably choose to skip the pain and to keep our ignorance. In His love God will not let us do this. God uses trials to make us grow up, just as a child must pass through the difficult days of adolescence to arrive at adulthood. The central struggle of the Christian life is to learn the true value of things that are intangible and largely invisible to us. The truly wise person will love the God he can't see, will follow the Jesus whom he has never met in the flesh, will long for the righteousness he doesn't have, will strive to enter the kingdom that has not yet arrived in its fullness. The really good stuff is hard to see, and even more so because our own sin clouds our thinking. How are we going to clear our heads in such an oppressive atmosphere? God knows; He is going to clear our minds with trials.

Two passages—Hebrews 12 and James 1—speak specifically of this aspect of Christian experience. That is, they tell us of God's intention to teach us wisdom through trials and the serious questions raised about the faith of anyone who remains a fool. In both passages three important points emerge:

1. *Foolish Readers*—In their foolish response to their current tribulations, the readers are acting like unbelievers, whatever they may have once said they believed.
2. *God's School of Hard Knocks*—They shouldn't be surprised that the life of a disciple can be difficult: God Himself has told us that He uses troubles to teach us wisdom.
3. *Immature or Unbelieving?*—Their present faithlessness does not prove that they are not saved. However, it does raise a serious question: Are they only immature believers or hardhearted rebels against God?

HEBREWS 12

Foolish Readers

Hebrews was written to Jewish Christians who were thinking about abandoning their belief in Jesus as the Messiah. Their disillusionment stemmed partly from their disappointment with Jesus Himself: a mortal human being who suffered and died a humiliating death. The author devotes much of the letter to showing that Jesus had to be human like us; His mortality, His sacrificial death were all necessary for Him to be our High Priest. Part of their disappointment, however, seemed to be not theological but personal. One might think that following the King of the Universe would bring ease and rewards. Instead, becoming Christians had brought them persecution and suffering. They seemed to be having second thoughts about a Messiah who suffered and in turn lets His disciples suffer.

God's School of Hard Knocks

In chapter 12 the author of Hebrews reminds his readers that nothing is unusual in the hardships they face; it would be foolish to abandon belief in Jesus because they, His disciples, were suffering. God has always dealt with His people in this way. The Old Testament heroes of the faith all suffered and persevered in their faith. Jesus Himself persevered through many sufferings and won glory in the end. Why would the followers of the Messiah be any different? What did they expect? They had forgotten that God has always made His intention clear: He disciplines all His children (Hebrews 12:6).

Such discipline is not a punishment, in the sense of "getting what we deserve." Jesus died on the cross for us to ensure we do *not* get what we deserve. "Discipline" here does not refer to punishment, but to the training of a child. Instruction, practice, correction—all these things a father uses to train his child; all these things God uses to train us. This training is not optional. As long as we live, God is going to teach us, and He is going to use difficult times to do it. Nothing gets our attention like trouble; our sluggish hearts will often wake up for nothing else.

> Our [earthly fathers] disciplined us for a short time as seemed best to them, but [God] disciplines us for our good, that we may share His holiness. All discipline for the moment seems not to be joyful, but sorrowful; yet to those who have been trained by it, afterwards it yields the peaceful fruit of righteousness. (Hebrews 12:10-11)

Trials are not designed to be pleasant; they are designed to train us, to mature us, to make us wise. The author of Hebrews does not spell out the dynamic of this process; he does not explain how perseverance through trials molds our character. But he does make one thing very clear: This painful discipline process is not a random misfortune that happens to a few unfortunate believers. It is the rule, not the exception. God shows His fatherly care the way any father does, by training His children in the ways of wisdom. And like any father, His training process at first can seem somewhat brutal and arbitrary to the child.

Immature or Unbelieving?
The author of Hebrews is worried about his readers. Instead of learning through their trials, instead of growing up and coming to terms with the deep beauty of the gospel, they are resentful toward God and ready to walk away from Jesus altogether. Their foolish hesitancy raises the most troubling questions about their

status before God; as the author of Hebrews warns them elsewhere, "How shall we escape if we neglect so great a salvation?" (Hebrews 2:3). Likewise, if they persevere through their trials, hold fast to Jesus as the Christ (Messiah), and thus grow in the maturity and stability of their faith, this would speak volumes about the reality of the work of God in their hearts.

The author of Hebrews is not denying that his readers are believers; he is raising the question, not answering it. Sometimes he speaks with a certain hopeful optimism about them (Hebrews 6:9). He evidently thinks that a genuine believer could still wrestle with folly and faithlessness for some time. Even their questioning the rock-bottom truth that Jesus is the Christ does not automatically mark them as children of darkness. But their situation is very serious. So far their trials have not led to perseverance and wisdom, but rather have pushed them to the brink of abandoning Jesus. In their trials they are facing the same choice they had when they first became Christians. Will they believe the gospel and hold fast to Jesus? This time, however, they understand better what that choice involves.

JAMES 1

Foolish Readers

We cannot understand the book of James if we do not recognize how worried James is about his readers. The letter sounds a sober warning from beginning to end. He reminds them that heeding "the Word" will save their souls, but to be a hearer of that Word without "doing" it is to be deluded. Such religion is worthless (James 1:21-27). To these readers James addresses his famous remarks about faith and works (which we will explore in the next chapter), telling them that a faith without works cannot save them (James 2:14-26). He rebukes them with, "You adulteresses, do you not know that friendship with the world is hostility toward God?" (James 4:4).

What were they doing that evoked such harsh language? James accuses them of fighting and murdering each other in their greedy pursuit of wealth (James 4:1-2). They were being persecuted by rich unbelievers, but this seemed to inspire in them only a desire to become rich themselves by whatever means. Throughout the letter, James reminds them that their rich oppressors, whom they envy so much, must lose all their wealth in the end. On the other hand, humble believers stand to inherit a kingdom that will make them truly blessed, truly to be envied. Why do James' readers curry favor with the rich and treat the poor with contempt? They have forgotten what they had once said they believed, that poor believers are "rich in faith and heirs of the kingdom which He promised to those who love Him" (James 2:5).

James sees many of his readers living lives totally out of step with the faith they say they have. James is forcefully asking them to confront a hard question: If you live every bit as foolishly as an unbeliever does, then in what sense do you "believe"?

God's School of Hard Knocks

James, like the author of Hebrews, portrays God as using trials to teach us wisdom.

> Consider it all joy, my brethren, when you encounter various trials, knowing that the testing of your faith produces perseverance. Now may perseverance have a perfect work, that you may be perfect and complete, lacking in nothing. But if any of you lacks wisdom, let him ask of God, who gives to all men generously and without reproach, and it will be given to him. (James 1:2-5*)

James' thought is a little difficult to follow here. As we saw in the last chapter, James speaks of the connection between the testing of our faith and perseverance. James goes on, however, to make it clear that more than testing is happening in a trial. The very process of persevering under trial changes us; it leads to our "perfection."

Perfection is a difficult idea to grasp. What does James mean that perseverance makes us "perfect"? He could mean the complete moral perfection that is the destiny of all believers; perseverance in this life leads to perfection in the next. Although this is certainly true theologically, it is not James' point in this passage. Rather, James is speaking of a "perfection" at which believers arrive in this life. He is speaking of *wisdom*.

The English word "perfect" is often not the best translation for the Greek word *teleios*, and the translation is particularly misleading in this context. This word does not mean "without flaw in every sense"—like Mary Poppins, "practically perfect in every way." Closer to the mark are ideas like "mature," "grown-up," "completed," "having arrived at the goal." The distinction is between that which has just begun versus that which has been completed, that which is implicit versus that which has been actualized. An adult is "perfect" in the way a child is not; an oak tree is "perfect" in a way an acorn is not. In fact, sometimes English Bibles translate *teleios* as "mature." Exactly the same word is used in Hebrews 5, which speaks of "the *mature*, who because of practice have their senses trained to discern good and evil" (Hebrews 5:14).

James believes faith is incomplete, immature, until it has worked its way into our attitudes and actions. A faith that has not yet had to make real-life choices is an untested faith—perhaps a faith in name only. It is one thing to say "I believe"; it is another thing to persevere in that belief, to embrace the consequences of that belief, and to live wisely in the light of the belief. For instance, James says Abraham's works "perfected" his faith (James 2:22). When God tested Abraham's faith, Abraham had to act on what he believed; as a result, faith became less abstract in Abraham's life. (It also demonstrated the reality of Abraham's faith, which we will discuss in the next chapter.) What God did with Abraham is His normal way of dealing with believers. James is saying essentially that perseverance leads to our maturity; it makes us grow up. An experienced, tested, mature believer is "perfect"—completed, grown-up, matured, wise—in a way an untested believer is not. James is concerned about his readers because their faith has not ripened into wisdom; they are greedy, worldly fools. His concern will only be relieved when their faith is "perfected" by actually affecting the way they think and act.

Immature or Unbelieving?

James' letter is a mixture of severe warning and gracious encouragement. He is asking his readers to look deep into their own hearts, but he is not pronouncing a sentence of damnation upon them. He writes because he hopes that some of his readers truly will have ears to hear. He tells them how God will give them wisdom generously, without reproach. He urges them to humble themselves before God and weep over their faithlessness. If they draw near to God, God will draw near to them. Perhaps some of his readers are just immature, still sorting things out in the midst of their trials. James clearly hopes that this is the case. Just as clearly, however, he cannot assure them that they indeed are saved because they are acting exactly like people who are not.

PERSPECTIVE ON THE PROCESS

God Is Not Being Arbitrary or Unkind

When we talk about God's discipline, and certainly when we *experience* God's discipline, we are sorely tempted to charge God with being arbitrary and mean. He could have spared us this suffering, but He didn't. It helps to remember what discipline is: the inevitable training a child must get on the journey to adulthood. I think of my daughter when she was very young and how she responded to my discipline—with screams of frustration, belligerent resistance, and heartfelt charges that I was being mean and unfair. She didn't understand yet how dangerous the things around her were. She couldn't see past the end of her nose, and she didn't know how to tell herself "no." She needed my training; the world is filled with things that could have killed her or wounded her or cost her dearly in later years. But she didn't understand, and so she was incredibly frustrated. She only knew something wonderful was being denied her.

God's children are truly like children. We don't realize how dangerous some of our toys are. We are like stubborn kids delightedly pulling glittery baubles out of a toxic waste dump; our playthings are deadly, but they are so much *fun*. The Bible sounds a constant note of warning very much like what a parent says to a child. Keep away from these things because they will kill you. Flee immorality; flee idolatry; flee youthful lusts; keep your life free from the love of money—such foolish and harmful desires plunge men into ruin and destruction; run away quickly. The author of Hebrews warns us that discipline is not joyful—and it isn't. But it is what we need.

Of course, God could have spared us from suffering by immediately transporting us to heaven. But God seems to think this process of trials is good for us. Not only do trials assure us of our real faith, but wisdom itself is a valuable commodity in a foolish world. We will profit from the struggle; to learn to love and to trust God in a world like this is worthwhile. Never again throughout eternity will we learn as much about the wages of sin as we are learning now; we are drinking Adam's cup of rebellion to the dregs. We are like children caught smoking behind the barn, and our Father is forcing us to smoke the whole pack. It is a nauseating experience from which great wisdom comes.

Biblical Wisdom Does Not Solve Life's Problems

Some people get the wrong idea that biblical wisdom is primarily intended to make life easier today. They think of some of the proverbs in the Old Testament and conclude that wisdom is intended to win us happiness and success in this life. Then they feel guilty because they don't feel "wise." They don't always know what to do. They don't know how to avoid suffering for themselves and their children. Shouldn't wise people have all the answers?

Wise people do not have all the answers. True, authentic, mature Christians will not always know what to do. We are not gaining that kind of wisdom. Biblical wisdom centers on the right values, the right hopes and desires for the future. In many ways a broken world like ours will forever pose problems Christians don't know how to solve. Nevertheless, we have real wisdom. True wisdom is learning to love what ought to be loved and to hate what ought to be hated. The wise person has a growing taste for righteousness, mercy, love, and justice; the wise person is also growing increasingly suspicious of the world's hollow promises. Truly wise people don't necessarily know how to solve the world's problems, but they are holding on with increasing tenacity to the One who does.

Failure Is Part of the Process

In this chapter I have tried to make a sobering but simple point: God's normal means of working with His people is to use troubles to teach them wisdom. If our lives are not characterized by wisdom, if we live like faithless and worldly fools, then the question cannot be avoided: Are we immature believers or enemies of God? This is what I understand the Bible to teach over and over again. I do not want to scare anyone, however, by implying that only those who have their lives "together" can be confident of salvation. That would be both unbiblical and unkind.

First of all, God's timetable for everyone's life is different. Some people learn important lessons quickly; others wrestle with God over the same issue for years. Some achieve a depth of wisdom apparent to all the world; some die quickly and show the world nothing. Nothing in the Bible (or in the experience of Christians throughout the ages) suggests that a uniform and speedy ascent to maturity is the only way God saves us. However, the Bible does say this: While I am on this earth, if my life contradicts my claim to believe, I cannot casually assume that I belong to God. For as long as I live, my continuing choices are significant indicators of my inner spiritual realities.

Secondly, mature believers are not free of moral struggle. Maturity means being deeply committed to the most important truths; it does not imply that we are free from the temptations of the flesh. If we are coming to understand the depth of our sin and the magnitude of God's grace, then we are wise. If we are coming to see God as real and loving and worthy of all our trust and loyalty, then we are wise. If we are coming to understand that nothing in this world compares with the inheritance God has promised His people, then we are wise. And if we are growing wise in these ways, then our lives will come to reflect this wisdom. Our values and commitments will center more and more on God, but this does not automatically free us from moral struggle and failure. Moral failure and maturity can and do go hand in hand.

CONCLUSION

Seeing the first sprouts of wisdom in ourselves should be profoundly encouraging; that is how the biblical authors saw it in the lives of their readers. We must not be like the pessimist who calls the glass half empty; that there is any water in the glass at all is a miracle. The dire warnings of Hebrews and James are addressed to people whose lives are profoundly and seriously compromised. At this point in their lives everything about them belies their initial "belief" in Jesus. We have no reason to believe that James would have written such a letter if he thought his readers were repentant, sorrowful believers who struggle against their own moral weaknesses. Instead, they are complacent and self-satisfied in their faithlessness; he tells them that they are laughing when they ought to be crying.

James reminded his very foolish readers that to those who lack wisdom, God gives wisdom generously and without reproach. In other words, even worldly, back-biting, short-sighted, self-serving people like themselves would receive wisdom from God, if indeed they were the sort who would trust Him. Perhaps the words in the Bible that strike the deepest chord with weak people like ourselves are found in Mark 9:24: The father of the boy possessed by a deaf and dumb spirit says to Jesus, "I do believe; help me in my unbelief." So must the Lord help us all. If we find evidence of a mature faith in our lives, we should thank God and not get cocky. If we discover how foolish and faithless we are, we should seek mercy and help from the fountainhead of all mercy and help. Our lifelong task is to invest our faith and trust in the Lord of life. Whether we feel strong or weak, wise or foolish, the right answer is always the same: We must turn to Him with whatever faith and understanding we have. "Draw near to God and He will draw near to you." Those who do this have the true wisdom, a deep-rooted wisdom that will grow all their lives.

CHAPTER EIGHT

Faith and Works

⌁

The Bible can leave us with puzzling and sometimes terrifying questions. One such question concerns the connection between faith and works. The puzzle is a theological one: How do we put together the biblical teaching on faith and works? On the one hand we know our works are tainted with evil and can never earn our salvation; that's why Jesus died on the cross. On the other hand, good works seem to be expected of every true Christian.

The Bible often talks about the difference between God's people and the rest of the world. That's the theological puzzle—in one sense works don't matter, and in another sense they matter very much.

We look to the Bible to tell us how sinners like ourselves find justification with God. This is what we most want to know. Not surprisingly, then, our first encounter with the following two verses can be disheartening:

> For we maintain that a man is justified by faith apart from works of the Law. (Romans 3:28)

> You see that a man is justified by works, and not by faith alone. (James 2:24)

If Paul and James can't get this straight, it's terrible news. We are lost in the wilderness, and we find our two guides fighting over the way home. And, of course, most of us have a sneaky preference for Paul over James. Compared with Paul and his liberating proclamation of grace, James can seem stern and demanding. It is as if Paul were running enthusiastically through the streets shouting, "Grace! Forgiveness! Eternal Life! It's all free, just have faith!" James, the dour elder brother, lumbers behind him, saying, "Ahem. Well, yes, it is 'free,' (beautiful words of course), but let's be realistic. By free we don't really mean 'free'—of course you are going to have to do good works."

Paul and James seem to disagree about the most important question of all. If Paul is right, then James seems to be a legalist; if James is right, then Paul seems to be an antinomian ("anti-law"). In these two verses we see one of the most obvious examples of the tension in biblical theology. Does salvation come in spite of my works or because of my works? Or, as strange as it might seem, could both be true?

Previous chapters have prepared us to begin answering these questions. We have seen that the Christian life is a process of rebirth, trial, and maturity. This is not an optional process. Every child of God has a new heart that welcomes the truths of God. The reality of this heart-change is tested in the crucible of life. As a result of these trials, over time believers grow in maturity and wisdom. Seen in this light, works take their proper place in the Christian life. We are not being asked to prove our innate moral perfection through our works; we couldn't do that. However, there is an unbreakable connection between what we do and what we truly believe. As we persevere and grow in our faith, we cannot help changing what we think and what we do.

THE SIGNIFICANCE OF WORKS

Before looking at Paul's and James' arguments, it will be helpful to consider the basic idea of "works." A work is an action of a human being. The Bible usually concentrates on deliberate actions, which say something about the will of the actor. If I stumble and accidentally push you into the path of an oncoming bus, I certainly have done something significant, but only in terms of the outcome; such a "work" says nothing about me (except that I am clumsy). If I deliberately push you, or if I risk my neck to pull you out of the way, then my "work" says something significant about me. What I do shows my values, beliefs, desires, and commitments.

At the heart of the biblical teaching about works is this simple but profound idea: What you are inside will show up in your actions. You will know a tree by its fruit. For believers, this cuts both ways. Our sin betrays itself in our deeds; that's why the gospel is such good news. But our sin is not the only thing that shows itself in our works. If we have a heart of faith, that will also be seen in what we do.

Suppose I am a fanatical fan of our current president of the United States. I am on the record as trusting everything he says. One day the President makes an amazingly silly announcement: "A space ship from Zargon is about to zap Eugene, Oregon, with a destructo ray." While others around me are saying, "He must be nuts," I insist, "The President wouldn't lie. If the President says so, then I believe it." Wouldn't my claim to trust him be suspect if I didn't leave town? What meaning does my statement, "I trust the President," have if I don't follow it up by actually and actively trusting him?

What we do reflects our inner realities. Thus, a biblical worldview tells us that two realities will appear in the "works" of believers. Since our moral characters are evil and flawed, our works reflect this; we do selfish, sinful things, betraying the evil in our hearts by our actions. Naturally we can't be justified by works because our works only condemn us. We cannot forget, however, that a believer's heart contains more than just sin. God has radically transformed believers' hearts. They have a new orientation toward God—new hopes and new longings and a new honesty. This "righteous" spirit will also show itself in our works. If we are truly honest about our sin, then we will act like contrite, humble people. If we truly trust God, we will act like people who trust God. If we long for His righteous kingdom, we will act like people who have such longings. Our works show our orientation, our commitments. If our actions show no evidence of this heart change, it is only right to ask whether the "faith" we claim is real. If we have faith, then why do our actions show no trace of it? If we believe the destructo ray is coming, why don't we leave town?

In their teaching on works, Paul and James each speak to a different issue. Paul addresses the question: "What do we deserve?" We cannot earn our salvation because our works betray the evil in our hearts. This is true for believers and unbelievers alike. James does not disagree with this. He addresses a different question altogether: "What do we believe?" What we truly believe will show itself in our works; in this sense the works of believers and unbelievers will differ in significant ways.

PAUL ON THE WORKS OF ABRAHAM

Upon first examination, the inconsistency between Paul and James seems to get worse, not better. Paul and James not only seem to disagree about faith and works; they also use the same piece of evidence to arrive at seemingly opposite conclusions. Both appeal to the life of Abraham as evidence; both appeal to the following statement from Genesis:

> Then [Abraham] believed in the LORD, and He reckoned it to him as righteousness. (Genesis 15:6)

Paul uses this verse to prove Abraham was justified by faith; James uses it to prove Abraham was justified by works. Careful examination of both Paul and James, however, shows their explanations of Abraham's life fit together very well. We will start with Paul.

In the book of Romans, Paul is answering objections raised by those Jews who have rejected the gospel altogether. They do not believe that Jesus is the Messiah. They particularly object to the idea that Gentiles can be saved without strict obedience to the Jewish Law—belief in Christ, apart from law-keeping, can't possibly be enough to save anyone.

In answering these objections, Paul focuses on Genesis 15:6 to help make and defend three points:

1. Obedience to Jewish religious rituals cannot in itself save anybody.
2. Our works are morally flawed, so we need mercy.
3. The person who has faith will be justified.

Obedience to Jewish religious rituals in itself cannot save anybody. Paul's Jewish opponents can't believe that God would accept an uncircumcised Gentile. In Romans 4:9-12, Paul points out that long ago God did justify an uncircumcised man: Abraham! Abraham was *called justified* in Genesis 15; Abraham was *circumcised* in Genesis 17. God's acceptance can't be conditioned on keeping the Law, for God justified Abraham before there was any law to keep. So Abraham was not justified by virtue of religious works.

Our works are morally flawed, so we need mercy. Paul's opponents have lost sight of the essentials: Keeping a ritual means nothing without true goodness. And goodness is our problem. Our works are morally flawed because our hearts are morally flawed. We cannot ask God for what we deserve; we can only hope He will be merciful. Paul appeals to Genesis 15:6 as evidence that Abraham received mercy, not justice.

> What then shall we say that Abraham, our forefather according to the flesh, has found? For if Abraham was justified by works, he has something to boast about; but not before God. For what does the Scripture say? "And Abraham believed God, and it was reckoned to him as righteousness." Now to the one who works, his wage is not reckoned as a favor but as what is due. But to the one who does not work, but believes in Him who justifies the ungodly, his faith is reckoned as righteousness. (Romans 4:1-5)

Paul does not specifically say Abraham was a sinner; he does

not specifically say Abraham received mercy. But he does prove
from Genesis that Abraham didn't get what he had coming to
him. God wouldn't have to "reckon" righteousness to Abraham
if he had already earned it through his works. God counted Abraham as righteous, even though he was not in fact righteous.

To make his point doubly clear, Paul immediately turns to
Psalm 32 as another example of justification apart from works:

> Just as David also speaks of the blessing upon the man to
> whom God reckons righteousness apart from works:
> "Blessed are those whose lawless deeds have been for-
> given, and whose sins have been covered. (Romans 4:6-7)

In the psalm, mercy for sin is clearly in view and Paul sees
Abraham's situation in exactly the same terms. Abraham did not
earn a righteous status with God because he was a sinner like
David. Instead, God accepted Abraham *in spite of* what his works
deserved.

The person who has faith will be justified. Paul's opponents
consider faith in Jesus an inadequate substitute for keeping the
law. Paul uses Genesis 15:6 to show that faith has always been the
doorway into God's favor: Religious works are inadequate;
morally perfect works are impossible; only faith in God's promises
puts us in His favor. Abraham heard God's promises that a child
from Abraham's own body would establish a great nation of blessing. Abraham believed God, and on that basis God declared him
righteous. Therefore faith in Jesus is not some new alternative to
law-keeping; the faith we have in Jesus is just the latest example
of the faith God has always required of His people.

In order to answer his opponents, Paul concentrates on the
question, "What do our works deserve?" Abraham provides the
evidence Paul needs to answer that question:

1. Abraham was not saved by religious works; no child
   of God will be either.
2. Abraham did not receive what his sinful works
   deserved but instead received mercy; all children of

God need such mercy.

3. Faith was the key to God's favor for Abraham, just as
it will be for all God's children.

Thus Paul teaches that we are not justified by "works." We
couldn't be because religious works are not enough, and morally
perfect works are beyond our capability.

JAMES ON THE WORKS OF ABRAHAM

To understand James, we must understand what he means by
"works." His topic is not ritual, religious works, nor is it morally
perfect works; rather, it is what we might call "works of faith."
Sooner or later, if we believe what we say we believe, our actions
will reflect our beliefs. A faith that does not act is not faith.

James sees Abraham as the great example of faith in action.
In order to follow James' thinking, we need to look at certain
milestones in Abraham's life. James' argument depends on the
chronological development of Abraham's understanding and
actions.

The Life of Abraham
God promised Abraham a land, a posterity, and a blessing
to the world.

> Now the Lord said to Abram, "Go forth from your coun-
> try, and from your relatives and from your father's house,
> to the land which I will show you; and I will make you a
> great nation, and I will bless you, and make your name
> great; and so you shall be a blessing; and I will bless
> those who bless you, and the one who curses you I will
> curse, and in you all the families of the earth shall be
> blessed." (Genesis 12:1-3)

This is the "Abrahamic Covenant." God promises Abraham
that he, Abraham, will found a nation in a new land, bringing
great blessing to Abraham and to the world. These are magnificent

and important words. Paul says that in them Abraham had the gospel preached to him (Galatians 3:8). Ultimately, the blessing that came through Abraham is the kingdom of Jesus Christ.

Abraham acted on God's promise, moving to the Promised Land.

> So Abraham went forth as the LORD had spoken to him. . . . And Abraham took Sarai his wife and Lot his nephew, and all their possessions which they had accumulated . . . and set out for the land of Canaan. (Genesis 12:4-5)

Abraham's response to God included a "work"; God said to go, and he went. Abraham, now in the Promised Land, was ready to found a great nation. But a great nation needs to start somewhere; for these promises to come true, Abraham needed to have a child. Abraham knew this very well, and later on he told God so.

Abraham asked God how the blessing could come without a child.

> After these things the word of the LORD came to Abram in a vision, saying, "Do not fear, Abram, I am a shield to you; your reward shall be very great." And Abram said, "O Lord GOD, what wilt Thou give me, since I am child-less, and the heir of my house is Eliezer of Damascus?" And Abram said, "Since Thou hast given no offspring to me, one born in my house is my heir." (Genesis 15:1-3)

In other words, Abraham asked, "How can I found a great nation and inherit the blessing you promised me if I don't have any kids?" God answered by making His promise more specific.

God promised Abraham a child of his own.

> Then behold, the word of the LORD came to him, saying, "This man will not be your heir; but one who shall come forth from your own body, he shall be your heir." And He took him outside and said, "Now look toward the

heavens, and count the stars, if you are able to count them." And He said to him, "So shall your descendants be." (Genesis 15:4-5)

Abraham now knew God was promising him at least one child of his own and through that child the promised blessings would come. In one of the key statements in Scripture, we are told of Abraham's response.

Abraham was justified by faith.

Then he believed in the LORD; and He reckoned it to him as righteousness. (Genesis 15:6)

Paul rightly points to this passage as describing Abraham's justification by faith. Abraham heard God's promise of blessing through his child, he trusted God to do it, and God accepted Abraham because of his faith. Note carefully that Abraham believed a specific promise, and the promise involved a child from his own body.

Paul's discussion of Abraham's life stops here, with Abraham trusting God and God justifying him because of it. James' argument, however, relies on succeeding events in Abraham's life. After Abraham fathers Ishmael with his wife's handmaiden, God gives him more specific information about the promise.

Abraham requested that his son Ishmael be the promised child.

And Abraham said to God, "Oh that Ishmael might live before Thee!" (Genesis 17:18)

Abraham now had exactly what God had promised: a child from his own body. Although Ishmael came through his wife's handmaid and not through his wife, still the child fit the requirements. Abraham asked God to bless Ishmael as the child of promise.

God specified Isaac as the child of promise.

But God said, "No, but Sarah your wife shall bear you a

son, and you shall call his name Isaac; and I will establish
My covenant with him for an everlasting covenant for his
descendants after him." (Genesis 17:19)

Not just any son from Abraham's body would fulfill God's
promise. Abraham and barren Sarah would have a child whom
they would name Isaac. Through him the blessings would come;
through him God would found a great nation, and would bless
all the nations of the earth.

After Isaac was born, God took Abraham through the piv-
otal experience of his life.

God tested Abraham.

Now it came about after these things, that God tested
Abraham, and said to him, "Abraham!" And he said,
"Here I am." And He said, "Take now your son, your
only son, whom you love, Isaac, and go to the land of
Moriah; and offer him there as a burnt offering on one of
the mountains of which I will tell you." (Genesis 22:1-2)

God put Abraham to the test. We will discuss the nature of
that test below; for now, note that the test concerned Isaac, the
child at the center of all God's promises. Abraham, in spite of
everything Isaac meant to him, obeyed God and attempted to
sacrifice him, being stopped at the last minute by the angel of
the Lord.

**God confirmed the promise because of Abraham's obedi-
ence.**

Then the angel of the LORD called to Abraham a second
time from heaven, and said, "By Myself I have sworn,
declares the LORD, because you have done this thing, and
have not withheld your son, your only son, indeed I will
greatly bless you, and I will greatly multiply your seed as
the stars of the heavens, and as the sand which is on the
seashore; and your seed shall possess the gate of their
enemies. And in your seed all the nations of the earth

shall be blessed, because you have obeyed My voice.
(Genesis 22:15-18)

Now the story gets really interesting. God had already promised these things to Abraham earlier in Genesis, and Abraham had believed them and had been accepted by God because of his belief. Yet, this later passage says God tested Abraham and accepted him because of his *obedience*. James is not the only one who sees Abraham finding God's favor through works—the angel of the Lord says exactly this to Abraham. What is going on? Is it fair for Paul to say Abraham was justified by faith apart from works? Is Paul cheating by ignoring Abraham's obedience in Genesis 22? Was Abraham justified by his faith or his works or both?

The Test
The answers to these questions lie in the nature of the test. God asked Abraham to sacrifice the life of his son. What was He testing? We can easily be misled by our emotional reaction to the idea of child sacrifice. The test might seem to be, "Just how low would Abraham sink for God?" This is not the point. Rather, God was testing Abraham's faith in the promises. In three stages Abraham had learned: (1) He would be the father of a great nation of blessing; (2) this nation would originate in a child from his own body; and (3) this child would be Sarah's as well and would be named Isaac. Finally Abraham had Isaac, the promised child, in his arms, and God was asking Abraham to give him back. Abraham was willing to do the apparently foolish act of offering his son because he believed these specific promises of God.

God was testing in Abraham the very faith in God's promises that Abraham had expressed earlier. This faith showed itself through Abraham's "work." As the author of Hebrews confirms, Abraham showed he understood and believed the promises God had made earlier:

By faith Abraham, when he was tested, offered up

Isaac; and he who had received the promises was offering up his only begotten son; it was he to whom it was said, "In Isaac your seed shall be called." He considered that God is able to raise men even from the dead; from which he also received him back as a type. (Hebrews 11:17-19)

Here the author of Hebrews gives us a fairly detailed commentary on *how* Abraham's faith and actions were related:

- When Abraham was tested, he offered Isaac "by faith."
- Abraham remembered that Isaac was the one and only child of promise, the one through whom God's promises would come.
- Abraham trusted God's promise concerning Isaac, and so believed that God would give him back. God had to raise Isaac; otherwise, how could He keep His promise?

Hebrews 11 is well-known as a roll call of the heroes of faith, the faith by which "men of old gained approval." Person after person is demonstrated to be a person of faith *by what he or she did*: Abel offered a better sacrifice; Noah built an Ark; Moses left Egypt; Rahab welcomed the spies; *and Abraham offered Isaac.* Abraham's "work," his action, in offering up Isaac was done "by faith." Specifically, Abraham believed God's promise that a nation of blessing would come through Isaac, and, because he believed, he was willing to give Isaac back *temporarily*. Isaac must live because God had promised. God was not testing Abraham's willingness to kill; He was testing Abraham's belief that Isaac would live just as God promised.

This "work" of Abraham's itself can't really be called a "good work," a "work of righteousness." He was still a sinner. God would not say to Abraham, "This proves you are morally perfect, deserving of my favor." It showed not Abraham's *goodness*, but his *faith*. In this situation Abraham might very well have yelled at Sarah, ignored her suffering at the potential loss of her child, gotten roaring drunk, or done any number of other selfish, sinful things. But whether he did these things or not, he did the most important thing—he trusted God.

Justified by Works

What James says about Abraham now becomes clearer:

> Was not Abraham our father justified by works, when he offered up Isaac his son on the altar? You see that faith was working with his works, and as a result of the works, faith was perfected; and the Scripture was fulfilled which says, "And Abraham believed God, and it was reckoned to him as righteousness," and he was called the friend of God. You see that a man is justified by works, and not by faith alone. (James 2:21-24)

James agrees with the angel of the Lord; he agrees with the author of Hebrews. The points James makes here line up very well with all that has been said about faith and works thus far:

- Abraham's faith, his belief in the promises God had made earlier, was "working with his works." He based his actions on his trust in God's promises. His works were neither blind obedience nor perfect goodness; they were actions arising from a real trust in God.
- Abraham's works "perfected" his faith. An "imperfect" faith is immature, untested, not yet acted upon, even though it may be a genuine saving faith. When the trials of life force us to confront our beliefs and act on them, our faith matures, is actualized, is "perfected." When Abraham said, "I believe," he meant it, but when God tested him, he experienced the reality of his faith, a trust so real he was willing to pick up a dreadful knife. He could never be the same man again. His faith was perfected.
- Abraham's works "fulfilled" the earlier (Genesis 15:6) Scripture. This statement, although confusing

at first, is the most important statement in James'
argument. What does James mean by "fulfill"?
"Abraham believed God" is not a prediction, so how
can Genesis 22 "fulfill" it? Although Genesis 15 tells
us Abraham heard the promise of a child from his
body and believed it, in a subtle way we wait for the
other shoe to drop. A change in beliefs begins as an
internal, invisible reality, but it promises a later
change in actions; that is the way life works. If
Abraham trusted God's magnificent promises, then
sooner or later he would act like someone who
believed them. Implicit in the statement "Abraham
believed God" are truths about Abraham that were
not yet "fulfilled," brought to fruition in their full
significance. When God tested Abraham in Genesis
22, the other shoe drops. We see the faith described
in Genesis 15 acting in Genesis 22. Thus the implicit significance of "he believed God" is fulfilled in
"Abraham stretched out his hand, and took the
knife to slay his son."

■ Abraham's works "justified" him. This of course is the
real stumbling block. Doesn't James listen when he
quotes Genesis 15:6, "it was reckoned to him as righteousness," which explicitly says Abraham was justified
by faith? Paul thinks Abraham was justified by faith,
and he uses Genesis 15:6 to prove it. Does James disagree? No, James *also* believes Genesis 15:6 is about
Abraham's justification by faith, and his whole argument depends on it. James' statement that Abraham
was "justified by works," is a shorthand summary of
his whole argument: (1) Abraham was justified by
faith, as described in Genesis 15:6; (2) Abraham
showed the reality of that faith through his later
actions; therefore, (3) Abraham was justified by an
active faith, a faith that did "work." Abraham was not
justified by a faith with *no* actions; he couldn't be. His
justification required works, because justification

requires true faith, and true faith *acts* a certain way.

Neither Genesis nor James tells us what would have happened if Abraham had said "no." We do know other biblical people of faith who made wrong choices at times. If Abraham had resisted God initially, that would not have been the end of the story. In fact, however, that is not what happened. The story of Abraham is a story of a faith demonstrated and confirmed through action. That is why it is of interest to James. His point is not that believers never fail under pressure; his point is that what we believe will sooner or later show itself in what we do.

James is fighting the idea that a person can have a totally invisible faith that leaves no mark on his or her actions. He is contrasting "talking" faith and "doing" faith. When James rejects "faith without works," it might sound like he is saying, "It is not enough to trust God; you have to do good works in addition." In the context of James' argument, however, "faith without works" means "claiming to trust without doing it," "believing the facts about Jesus without actively embracing them."

James is not adding works as a new condition to Paul's "justification by faith"; he is saying the faith that justifies us has a tangible effect on our lives. To say, "I'm a Christian," is not enough. Faith arises out of a change in the way we look at the world, and when our worldview changes, so do our actions. Such a change doesn't make us *good* people now; it makes us *believing* people now. For James, "faith alone" is an empty claim to have faith when in reality a person's "works" show that the belief hasn't penetrated the heart.

CONCLUSION

Because moral struggle and failure continue throughout the Christian life, a misunderstanding of James can fill us with unnecessary fears. We can find ourselves constantly plagued by the thought that our works are not good enough. James does not mean for us to do this; he is not calling into question the graciousness of the gospel. We already know that our works are not good enough to earn salvation; Paul explained this to us, and James is not contradicting him. God is not taking away with one hand what He gave with the other.

Instead of being threatening, what James adds to Paul's teaching about works is helpful and revealing. Paul has taught us to see the moral imperfections in our works, the impossibility of being as good as we should. James reminds us that, as imperfect as they are, our works also reveal something about our beliefs, values, and commitments. He shows us one penetrating example: the life of Abraham. Abraham believed God's specific promise, and his actions showed the reality of that belief. I would argue that this connection between our inner beliefs and our outer behavior is the driving force behind most biblical exhortations. The Bible is not calling us to prove our moral perfection; it is calling us to act on our beliefs. A belief that hasn't acted is a belief that has not yet shown that it exists.

What does this look like in the Christian life? How is a believer in Christ asked to "offer up Isaac" today? We turn to that question next.

/ CHAPTER NINE /

As We Forgive Our Debtors

Most people would balk at the idea that Christians are uniquely characterized by "good works." Every day people of all faiths (and no faith) perform acts of kindness and charity. All kinds of people have deliberately chosen low-paying jobs to work with the poor or to defend the environment; many of them are atheists who look with contempt on the superstition of religion. The lives of many Christians look shamefully self-centered when compared to some of their nonChristian neighbors. When we consider all this, what are we to make of the connection James makes between faith and works? When many nonChristians are dedicating themselves to the welfare of the community, in what sense do works mark a believer as a believer?

First of all, we shouldn't be surprised that unbelievers do many good things in this world. The Bible tells us, and experience confirms, that all human beings start out with a basic knowledge of right and wrong. Being sinners doesn't mean that every single act we commit is as bad as it could be. All people do many good things throughout their lives because they are made in the image of God and because they have a certain amount of empathy for other people's troubles. But because we are sinners, none of us is nearly good enough. All of us, Christian and nonChristian alike, fail to love God and our neighbor

139

as we should. The "good works" of nonChristians merely show that they, like all human beings, have an ingrained understanding of the law of God, even if they deny that God exists. Both Christians and nonChristians do some good things; both Christians and nonChristians fail to be as good as they should.

Something very different is involved, however, when James speaks of "faith and works." He says that when a belief has truly taken hold of our minds and hearts, it will affect the way we do things. The Bible does not so much call us to "good works" as to "distinctively believing works." Remember the example of Abraham: a specific kind of belief (that God would bless him through Isaac) led to a specific kind of action (willingness to give Isaac back temporarily). As believers, the gospel confronts us with issues very different from those of the unbelievers around us:

- To believe the gospel we must confront the truth that God exists and that He is good and merciful and loving, the one to be trusted above all others.
- To believe the gospel we must confront the truth that we are guilty and morally ugly because of our sin.
- To believe the gospel we must confront the truth that nothing in this world is as valuable as the freedom from sin and death that God has promised us.

As these particular truths (and others) capture our thinking, the way we live our lives will change. "Works" in the Christian sense are an outworking of specific beliefs that are very different from those of unbelievers. Atheists' lives may show an instinctive understanding of human compassion, but they will not show a love and trust of God; they will not show a knowledge that their lives have earned them a place in hell; they will not show a growing passion for God's promises.

Most of the commands in the New Testament, I would argue, are applications of our uniquely Christian beliefs to specific situations. Do you say you believe that God is trustworthy? Great, here is your chance to actually trust Him. Do you say you know that you are a morally unworthy sinner? Great, here is your chance to embrace that truth in your actions. Do you say you really want the salvation found in God's kingdom? Great, here is your chance to make that choice in the midst of real life. To demonstrate what I mean, we will look at one specific command—the command to forgive others. I have chosen this example for three reasons:

1. Because of the demanding nature of this command, many have tried to explain it away as being totally unconnected with salvation. This is not true, and it is important that we understand this.
2. The New Testament teaching on forgiveness provides us with a great explanation of how what we believe is connected with what we do.
3. The command to forgive is of fundamental importance because it is rooted in a life-and-death issue we all must confront.

THE DYNAMIC OF FORGIVENESS

In earlier chapters we have explored how God uses trials both to confirm and to strengthen our faith. In a trial, our life circumstances force us to think about some aspect of the gospel, probing our true beliefs and desires. Our perseverance in holding fast to the gospel demonstrates the reality of our faith and causes our personal understanding of the gospel to grow. The result is wisdom, a new and better way of thinking about life, which leads to a change in our behavior. If instead a person's life shows a stubborn refusal to believe the gospel actively, serious questions are raised about that person's faith.

As we have also explored in earlier chapters, one of the truths implicit in the gospel is the hard truth about our own guilt. The gospel announces salvation for sinners; to embrace the gospel wholeheartedly means admitting that our guilt is as great as the gospel says it is. However, this is not something we admit easily. God may use trials to force us to deal with our own guilt, just as He does other gospel truths. But how would this happen? What sort of a trial tests whether I am humble or self-righteous? What kind of situation demands that I think about my own moral guilt? The Bible tells us of a powerful test of our own self-concept: How do we respond when we are called upon to forgive others?

All human beings live according to a dishonest double standard. When others sin against us, we can think of little else but the wrong and hurt and evil of what they did. On the other hand, when we sin against others, we find it easy to excuse, to defend, and to downplay our offenses. We are self-centered people. When justice is in our favor, we want justice; when mercy is in our favor, we want mercy. This tendency shows itself in the most trivial and the most serious aspects of life. I have seen this in my own life so often it has taken on a tragicomic flavor. I have lost count of how many times I catch myself being irritated by another person's actions, only to realize I do exactly the same things myself. When I mess up, I want you to be tolerant; when you mess up, I want you to stop it.

The gospel demands that we abandon the double standard. If we take the gospel seriously, it will not let us downplay our own guilt; we are so morally unworthy that it took the death of Christ Himself to pay the penalty. When we face the choice to forgive others, we are confronting that double standard directly. If I condemn the one who has sinned against me, how can I expect to escape condemnation myself? When struggling with whether to forgive others, it is as if God is speaking to us like this:

> Look at the evil this man has done to you. You are right to be upset. This man has been unloving; this man has shown contempt for Me; this man has done evil and deserves to be condemned. But what do you deserve? Will you call down the lightning from heaven on his head? If you do, what will keep it from striking you at the same time? Has he been unloving? You cannot begin to count the times you have been unloving in your life. Did he show contempt for a holy God? Think of all the

times you have ignored and distrusted and disobeyed Me. Is he evil? Are you trying to tell Me that you are not? When you look into the eyes of your enemy, you are looking into your own eyes. There is no difference; you are both guilty. Are you willing to see your own sins in the light of his? I have no double standard. Do you demand justice? You will receive justice, and you won't like it. Do you want mercy? You are as guilty as your enemy; if sins like yours can be forgiven, then so can sins like his.

Jesus Teaches on Forgiveness

The Unforgiving Servant

Jesus confronts our evil double standard most forcefully in the parable of the unforgiving servant (Matthew 18:21-35). In the process, He gives the best explanation found anywhere of what is at stake when we face the choice to forgive.

The servant in this story owes an astronomically large amount of money to his master. Jesus deliberately makes the figure impossibly huge; no servant could possibly run up—or repay—such a debt in real life. In a last desperate plea, the servant begs the master for more time to repay the debt. What else can the servant do? The master's response is generous beyond the servant's wildest dreams—the master forgives the total debt. The master loses a fortune; the servant is free from all obligation. Jesus paints an incredibly compelling picture—the servant has gone from total despair to total release. His heart should sing with joy because his master has been so kind to him. If any man in the world should understand the value of mercy over justice, this servant should. It seems impossible that his head would have any thought except how sweet mercy is.

What the servant does next in the story is meant to seem impossible. He refuses to forgive another servant who owes him a couple of bucks. It is as if a man lost in the desert, parched and dying, were kindly given a drink of clear water; then he turns and knocks the cup from another dying man's hands. How can this servant treat his fellow servant this way? How can he have forgotten how the burden of his own debt crushed him? How can he have forgotten how the master's mercy saved him from the pit and gave him new life? Naturally the master is outraged. How can this servant swagger around demanding justice? If he wants justice, then he will get justice. The crushing demands of justice come down on the servant again, and this time there is no escape.

Jesus has shown us in this story the connection between forgiving others and our own self-perception. If we truly believe the gospel, then we know ourselves to be like this servant. We owe a debt to God's justice that we could not repay in a million lifetimes. That Jesus would sacrifice Himself to free us from this debt is an act of generosity and mercy almost beyond comprehension. When we start to see how huge our own guilt problem is, then we can start to get perspective on other people's sins. Yes, they are guilty; so am I. I hate the things they have done, but I hate what I have done as well. They need mercy, just as I do.

In the story, a huge disparity exists between what the servant owes the master and what the servant himself is owed. This is not incidental but essential. If I were honest with myself, this is how my own sins ought to feel in comparison with others' sins against me. I have lived with myself my entire life; I have felt the mountain of debt I owe God's justice mount day by day and hour by hour. How many days have I spent ignoring God, accusing God, distrusting God, disobeying God? How many times have I put my own interests above those of others? If my brother sinned against me as many times as seventy times seven, he still couldn't owe me as much as I owe God.

The Same Measure
Jesus appeals to this same logic in the following passage from the Sermon on the Mount:

> "Do not judge lest you be judged yourselves. For in the way you judge, you will be judged; and by your standard of measure, it shall be measured to you." (Matthew 7:1-2)

At first glance, this passage might seem to speak to a different issue from forgiveness. "Not judging" and "forgiving" may sound like two different things. First, therefore, we should determine what Jesus means by "do not judge."

In today's American culture, which puts a premium on tolerance, "do not judge" is often interpreted as "do not presume to see anything wrong with what anyone else is doing." We don't have to look far to see that Jesus couldn't possibly mean that. We are supposed to be discerning, carefully distinguishing between good and evil. We are supposed to reprove our brother when he sins (Matthew 18:15). Paul urges us to restore humbly the one caught in a trespass, which means first of all we must discern that a wrong has been committed (Galatians 6:1). If by "judge" we mean "discern evil and call it what it is," then not only are we permitted to judge, we are commanded to.

In the Bible, "to judge" usually means much more than merely "to discern." To judge is "to pass sentence," "to condemn," "to play judge, jury, and executioner." When I judge, I take on myself what is God's prerogative alone: the right to determine what another person deserves. (God *has* given the State the right to judge social crimes, but that is another issue.) When I condemn another person in my heart and treat that person as harshly as I think he deserves, then I have "judged" him. "Judging," therefore, is essentially the opposite of "forgiving." If I have decided that I cannot treat you well because you deserve my contempt, then I am refusing to forgive you; I am judging you.

Jesus says that "by your own standard of measure it will be measured to you." Once again, as in the parable of the unforgiving servant, Jesus attacks the double standard. It is as if all our lives we carry a backpack with two scales: with one we measure others; with the second we measure ourselves. When the day of judgment comes, we hand God the scale by which we judged ourselves. "No," He says, reaching into our pack, "we'll use this other one." If we spend our lives insisting on condemnation for others' offenses, then we have bought condemnation for ourselves.

Jesus goes on to ask, "Why do you look at the speck in your brother's eye, but do not notice the log that is in your own eye?"

146 / *Faith at Work*

(Matthew 7:3). We have encountered this kind of extreme discrepancy before: the servant who owed a fortune and was himself owed a pittance. Jesus' analogy becomes more powerful if we stop to think, as I believe He means us to do, about the last time we had a speck in our eye. Everything stops; the pain is so intense that we abandon all other matters while we deal with it. Now imagine a huge, splintery log poking into your eye. How could you possibly ignore it or be more concerned about the speck in someone else's eye? This picture is meant to be ludicrous, and it is equally ludicrous to concentrate on others' faults while downplaying our own. If we were not so intent on ignoring our own guilt, our own offenses against God and our neighbors would seem to us like that log in the eye.

The gospel shows us Christ hanging on a cross and says, among other things, "this is what you deserve." When we say we believe this gospel, we are agreeing with God's assessment of our lives. However, this can be a fairly abstract concept at first. Having to forgive someone else takes the abstraction of our own guilt and forces us to deal with it. We find it easy to downplay our own sins before God, but we easily see the guilt of other people's sins against us. Jesus is forcing us to put the two side by side, to agree with Him that the guilt of our sins against God is even greater than that of those who have sinned against us. Our willingness to forgive others becomes the sign that our own sins have stopped being abstract to us, that we are willing to look into the eyes of another sinner and see ourselves.

Does He Mean It?
In passages like the ones we just examined, Jesus says that if we don't forgive, we will not be forgiven. Does this mean what it sounds like? Is Jesus saying that the forgiveness of my sins, my salvation, is dependent on whether I forgive others? My answer is, "Yes, but." Yes, the issue in these passages is salvation, but we need to be careful lest we make Jesus' teaching more demanding than He intends.

Salvation is the issue. In the parable of the unforgiving servant, for instance, the servant owed an impossible, astronomical debt. Can we doubt that Jesus means this debt to represent the full load of our guilt before God, the guilt which condemns us to hell? We should also pay attention to how the parable ends:

> And his lord, moved, with anger, handed him over to the torturers until he should repay all that was owed him. So shall My heavenly Father also do to you, if each of you does not forgive his brother from your heart. (Matthew 18:34-35)

The servant is handed to the torturers, still owing every cent to his master. Could this analogy represent anything other than the eternal condemnation that will come upon all whose sins are not forgiven? Justified, saved people do not go to some heavenly equivalent of the torturer's dungeon, do they? Neither should we think that "until he should repay" implies some sort of limited sentence. On the contrary, the debt this servant owed was so big that he never could repay it. His sentence holds no hope of reprieve.

Remember Peter. Having established that Jesus is speaking of salvation, we are still left with many questions. If I am currently unforgiving, does that mean I am not saved? What happens if I am trying to forgive someone, but I can't? What if I die before I have a chance to deal with the resentments I still harbor? Just how stringent a requirement is this? These questions don't just apply to forgiveness; they are relevant to every command we find in the Bible. How much room is there for failure?

We can make a good start toward answering these questions by considering another command of Jesus. He told His disciples:

> "Everyone therefore who shall confess Me before men, I will also confess him before My Father who is in heaven. But whoever shall deny Me before men, I will also deny him before My Father who is in heaven." (Matthew 10:32-33)

This is straightforward and easy to understand. Clearly salvation is in view; if Jesus denies us before His Father, we are lost. And it is easy to see the connection between this command and saving faith; if we believe in Jesus, surely at least we ought to say so. What Jesus says sounds blunt, categorical, and admitting of no exceptions.

What, then, shall we make of Jesus' close disciple, Peter? In one of the great trials of his life, Peter gave in to his fears and denied Jesus three times. Peter did exactly what Jesus told him he must not do: He denied Jesus before men. Is Jesus going to deny Peter before the Father? Not a chance; we know that Jesus reaffirmed Peter's place of leadership among the disciples. And we know that Peter in fact went on to show the strength and tenacity of his faith through many trials, ending with his execution.

How shall we explain the seeming discrepancy between what Jesus said and what happened to Peter? It is only a problem if we think of commands as a "one strike and you're out" situation. The evidence of Peter's life suggests, however, that God does not think in those terms at all. People are complex. A genuine faith does not immediately banish all other feelings and motivations. Peter loved Jesus, but he was also terrified by the events of that horrific night. What he did was wrong, disloyal, and faithless, but it was only one step in a longer journey. In the end, Peter didn't try to justify what he had done; he wept.

Faith is not a one-time event, but a decision we must make and remake in the trials of life. Jesus tells us what is at stake in those trials; He does not give us a checklist of activities we must perform to be saved. He means His commands to be seen in the long term, over the course of a person's entire life. Believing in Jesus ultimately involves believing in Him actively, choosing to believe Him in the face of personal cost or tempting distractions. But there is plenty of room for periods of struggle and failure — even *long* periods.

But what happens if we die before we can "prove" ourselves? Remember that God is not asking us to pass a qualifying test. Our trials are for our education, not God's. Our works are an important indicator that God is at work, but they do not save us. When we come before God, He will know better than we do ourselves whether our cry for salvation came from the heart. At the end of our lives, those we leave behind must be content to live with their questions. If we never resolve our bitter condemnation of others, we will certainly not leave behind an encouraging sign of our salvation. In the end, however, God will make known the true story; with that everyone must be content.

CLARIFICATION

Forgiveness is a very challenging topic, and whenever I teach on it people ask many questions. It seems good, therefore, to make clear what I am not saying, as well as what I am.

Forgiving Is Not Forgetting

Many counselors would urge us to find inner peace by forgiving others. The kind of "forgiveness" that many speak of, however, is often worlds apart from what Jesus means. Essentially they call us to rewrite history, to pretend it didn't happen, to stuff the pain and to forget. We achieve forgiveness by tricking ourselves into thinking there was nothing to forgive. This approach is attractive since it can pour oil on troubled waters and make everybody feel better. However, this kind of "forgiveness" has nothing to do with the teaching of Jesus.

Jesus is not asking us to deny the hurt and pain caused by others; He is not asking us to pretend they are not guilty. When I forgive you, I don't make less of your guilt; I make more of my own. I am a servant who owes a gazillion-dollar debt; I have a massive log in my eye. I know you are guilty, but I believe in a mercy that is bigger than your guilt toward me; it is even bigger than my guilt toward God.

Forgiving Is Not Based on Self-Hatred

Many reject the Christian teaching on forgiveness because, they argue, it promotes a terrible and destructive self-image. They hear Jesus saying that, in order to forgive others, we must see ourselves as worthless slime. Distinguishing between "morally guilty" and "worthless" is therefore very important. Every human being is a truly significant creation, made in the image of God.

We are not garbage; we are a defaced masterpiece. As sinners, we are guilty before a Holy God and have earned His wrath, but we are not *nothing*.

Jesus' teaching on forgiveness can be particularly hard for those who have been abused as children. For them, understanding both of the previous points is essential: (1) Forgiving is not forgetting; and (2) forgiveness is not based on self-hatred. Those who are victims of abuse often wrestle with feelings of worthlessness: "He was right to abuse me because I don't deserve to be loved." A person who has been sinned against won't make any progress toward true forgiveness until he realizes that the abuser did great evil, and that he as the "victim" is just as significant and worthy of love as anyone else. Only when the one who was hurt by another can see the abuser's guilt and his own worth is he ready to tackle the question of forgiveness. Yes, the one who was damaged is valuable and significant, and he should not have been treated that way. However, we are all still self-centered rebels against God, and in that sense the "victim" is just as guilty as the one who abused him — guilty of sinning against God, not guilty of the sin that was committed against him. God does not want any of us to despise ourselves; He wants us to see honestly that we are significant creatures who are corrupted, like everyone else, with the stain of sin. When we see that, then real forgiveness can happen, with no forgetting and no self-hatred.

Forgiving Is Not Moral Perfection

It is helpful to recognize that the Bible portrays two different kinds of "forgiveness" for us to consider:

Jesus Himself is the model for the first kind of forgiveness — the forgiveness that comes from a perfectly loving heart. Jesus showed the way on the cross, by asking God to forgive His killers. The motivation for forgiving them did not come from His knowledge of His own sins. He had no sins; if Jesus were to call down justice upon every sinner in the world, He Himself would escape unscathed. He forgave them because of His deep and flawless love.

When Jesus tells us to "love our enemies," He is calling us to follow Him in pursuing God's high moral call—to love our neighbor as ourselves. There is no chance, however, that we will do this perfectly. We can't even love our friends as well as we ought. Even with the people we care about most, we are often short-tempered, selfish, and self-centered. Will we do better with our enemies? God is not asking us to earn our salvation through our morally perfect love.

The parable of the unforgiving servant presents a second model of forgiveness: the refusal to condemn because we know that we ourselves deserve condemnation. This kind of forgiveness comes not from our perfect love, but from our own self-perception as sinners. Our love for our enemies—for anyone—is probably less than perfect. But the big question is this: Do we *condemn* our enemies? Are we calling down curses on them in our heart, all the while ignoring the curses we deserve? Although loving and forgiving perfectly is beyond our grasp, we show the reality of God's work in our hearts by our willingness to see others' sins in the light of our own.

CONCLUSION

Some commandments in the Bible present us with God's perfect moral will, the impossibly high standard for which we should constantly strive. "Love your neighbor as yourself" is a good example of this kind of command. However, many of the Bible's commands, especially in the New Testament, have a very different purpose. They tell us, "You say you believe the gospel; here is your real-life opportunity to believe it again." If we were to examine them, we would see how this is true for many biblical exhortations: giving a cup of water in Jesus' name; confessing Jesus in the face of persecution; fleeing from the love of money; and many others. As we have seen, the command to forgive belongs in this list. The Bible makes two things very clear: (1) Belief in the gospel is tied to our knowledge of our own guilt and need for forgiveness; and (2) when I exercise Christian forgiveness, I am confirming through my actions my belief in my own guilt. Forgiving others is one arena in which a living faith works itself out over time. If we will not forgive, we must ask the question whether we ourselves have been forgiven—or want to be.

PART FOUR

CRUCIAL QUESTIONS

CHAPTER TEN

Can Christians Conquer Sin?

—

Joe's pastor is a kind man who would give the shirt off his back for any of his flock, but he doesn't talk about sin much. In his sermons, he portrays the good news as God's liberating power to "be all that you can be," and his favorite verse is, "I can do all things through Him who strengthens me" (Philippians 4:13). Joe's Christian friends have a very triumphalist attitude toward sin. Whenever Joe tries to talk with them about moral failure, they encourage him to resist a defeatist and pessimistic attitude. In this situation, Joe has trouble finding anyone with whom he can be honest about his own struggles.

So Joe is intrigued by the idea that believers are still "sinners" and that they will continue to struggle with sin their entire lives. Joe doesn't find this idea defeatist; he finds it encouraging. Maybe his own struggles are a natural part of the Christian life after all. But then why do many Christians teach and believe in victory over sin? Doesn't the Bible sound pretty optimistic about the defeat of sin? Joe has been counseled many times to "know, reckon, and yield," or to "walk by the Spirit," as a technique for overcoming temptation. How can he sort all this out?

The topic of the Christian's struggle with sin deserves at least another book. To answer the questions involved takes us into some of the most complex and controversial passages in the Bible. Still, we can't leave Joe's questions entirely unanswered. I believe that victory over sin is a future hope, not a present reality. This chapter is a broad overview of my position.

THE NATURE OF OUR VICTORY

It may seem problematic to keep insisting that believers are still sinners. The New Testament doesn't use such language very often. Doesn't that suggest that this is the wrong self-concept for believers? To address that question, we have to reconsider the way the Bible uses words like "sinner."

We've already seen that the children of God have a new rightness about their hearts. Their hearts now trust God, admit sin, and so on. This represents a partial reversal of the problem of sin inherited from Adam and Eve. Completely corrupt hearts do not trust God; completely corrupt hearts do not admit their own corruption. The miracle of faith is indeed a moral revolution. Something evil in us kept us from admitting the truth about God; that evil has been removed. I believe this is why Paul speaks of our "washing":

> He saved us, not on the basis of deeds which we have done in righteousness, but according to His mercy, by the washing of regeneration and renewing by the Holy Spirit. (Titus 3:5)

We have been cleansed; that is, we have been reborn and renewed by the Holy Spirit. Since a certain kind of evil has lost its foothold in our hearts, it might seem appropriate to remove believers from the category of "sinners." And, in fact, sometimes the Bible does that very thing. The "sinners," the "wicked," are those who turn away from God in rebellion and unbelief:

> "So it will be at the end of the age; the angels shall come forth, and take out the wicked from among the righteous." (Matthew 13:49)

In order that they all may be judged who did not believe
the truth, but took pleasure in wickedness.
(2 Thessalonians 2:12)

And if it is with difficulty that the righteous is saved,
what will become of the godless man and the sinner?
(1 Peter 4:18)

. . . To execute judgment upon all, and to convict all
the ungodly of all their ungodly deeds which they
have done in an ungodly way, and of all the harsh
things which ungodly sinners have spoken against
Him. (Jude 15)

We catch glimpses in passages like these of what distin-
guishes believers from "the wicked." The people of God do
believe the truth; they do not take pleasure in wickedness; they
are not godless; they do not speak harsh things against their Savior. Believers are "righteous" because something is right about
their hearts, and this rightness shows itself in their beliefs and
actions. Unbelievers are "sinners" because their hearts are sinfully hardhearted and rebellious, and so they turn from God and
the things of God. In this sense, every true believer has victory
over sin.

However, I know that many would say I have not gone
far enough. The Christian life, they would argue, is a life of
power and victory; believers can overcome all moral failure
and achieve true sinlessness if they choose to do so. There are
many different theological flavors of this belief—different
explanations of when and how this victory is achieved—but
most agree on two points: (1) Believers have the power to
conquer temptation and avoid deliberate sin; and (2) not all
believers do conquer sin, but only those who choose to avail
themselves of this power. (I will use the term "triumphalism"
to refer to any theological system that maintains some version of these two points.) Put another way, the two important
questions are these:

1. Can believers, struggling with moral weakness, expect to find a power, a technique, that will lift their lives to a higher level of moral victory?
2. Are there two kinds of Christians, those who choose to appropriate this power and those who don't?

Triumphalism answers "yes" to both these questions; I answer "no."

Sin in Its Many Flavors

Sometimes debates about triumphalism bog down over competing definitions of sin. In order to make clear the senses in which we do and do not conquer "sin" in this life, let's consider a recent experience of Joe's. Joe had a crummy time at the Bible study last week. He was feeling low about some humiliating mistakes he had made that day at work. At the study he attempted to make several comments, but each time Charlie contradicted him. Joe thought Charlie was the most irritating know-it-all he had ever met, and so Joe was steaming inside. The third time Charlie said something, Joe started to argue back—first timidly, then vigorously, and finally with a hostility apparent to everyone. As it happens, Charlie was right and Joe was wrong, but Joe was too stubborn to admit it. On the way home, Joe's wife pointed out how unfair he had been to Charlie; Joe responded with an icy sarcasm that left her speechless.

In bed that night, Joe replayed the scene over and over in his head, thinking of all the killer put-downs he could have used on Charlie. Not until the next morning could Joe simmer down enough to admit he had been a jerk. He cringed when he thought of what he had said (and his fantasies about what he could have said). He apologized to his wife, and then, in a moment of godly courage, called Charlie and asked if they could talk over lunch.

There are (at least) six different senses in which we could speak of Joe's "sin":

1. *Sin as a violation of a known commandment.* We must be clear about one thing—what Joe did is sin. Some forms of triumphalism have a minimalist definition

of sin: Sin is only the specific violation of a known commandment. Joe didn't murder, commit adultery, or break the Sabbath, so he's okay. They would say that what Joe did here was just "human nature," not sin. However, the Bible clearly does not leave us this option. Jesus told us that not just murder, but hateful words and thoughts make us guilty before God. We are to love our neighbor as ourselves; we are even to love our enemies. Joe acted in selfish hostility, not love.

2. *Sin as evil actions.* Joe's actions were sinful. He said hurtful and selfish things to Charlie and his wife. He left the world an uglier place than it was before he spoke.

3. *Sin as evil attitudes.* Joe's attitudes were sinful. In his heart he resisted the truth because it made him feel uncomfortable. Even if Joe had managed to avoid saying anything to Charlie or his wife, his ugly thoughts would have shown him to be a sinner.

4. *Sin as evil impulses.* Joe's impulses were sinful. That is, he has an inner drive, an instinct, that tells him his own needs are more important than anyone else's. He is predisposed to think more of himself than of God or his neighbor. Even if Joe had managed to escape his bad attitude toward Charlie, it would only be by fighting against his own selfish inner voice.

5. *Sin as unbelieving attitudes.* Certain aspects of Joe's attitudes were not "sinful," as the Bible sometimes uses the word. His heart is "honest and good" in the sense that Jesus meant. He was willing to acknowledge his own evil. He grieved over his own selfishness. He called out to God in trust for mercy and help.

6. *Sin as unbelieving actions.* Certain aspects of Joe's actions were not "sinful," as the Bible sometimes uses the word. His genuine faith ultimately motivated him to act. He apologized to his wife. He called Charlie and tried to make amends and build some bridges.

In the light of these distinctions, then, here is what I am saying about "victory over sin" in the Christian life:

■ Joe's life, even in this episode, shows the signs of the true victory at work in his life. Joe is a victor for many reasons: He loves and trusts God; he can be honest about his own hurtful failings; he is striving after what is good and right; he longs for the day when his heart will be free of the selfishness and weakness that plague him every day of his life. Because of the work of God's Spirit in his life, Joe can expect to make progress. At the next Bible study, after having talked things over with Charlie, Joe may find himself more thoughtful and compassionate toward Charlie. Joe is being taught the truth by a Master Teacher.

■ In many important senses, however, Joe will not find victory over sin in this life. He will not lose his own evil impulses. He has no guarantee of freedom from evil attitudes. He has no guarantee of freedom from evil actions. Joe is still inclined to put his own interests above others'; there is nothing he can do to guarantee that he will not think and act selfishly again. No technique, no power exists that will free Joe from the struggle with his own self.

THE INTERPRETIVE ISSUES

Triumphalism and I come to different conclusions because of two fundamental interpretive disagreements:

1. Certain key biblical passages (we will examine a few below) describe a moral change in the lives of believers. Triumphalism equates this moral change with sinlessness; I believe this is an interpretive mistake. These passages do speak of real changes, but those changes are in our values, perceptions, convictions, goals, beliefs, and the actions which result from these—everything having

to do with Christian maturity. A genuine, growing faith, however, is not the same as the power to overcome all moral weakness in our lives.

2. These same key passages are clearly distinguishing between two different kinds of people: those who evidence this moral change and those who don't. Triumphalism sees the two groups as defeated Christians versus victorious Christians. Again, I think this interpretation has seriously missed the point. Where triumphalism sees two classes of *Christians*, I see two kinds of *people*: believers and nonbelievers; children of light as opposed to children of darkness.

I have selected three representative passages to illustrate the interpretive issues involved. Each of these passages deserves more discussion than we can afford here, but what follows should make clear my general approach.

The Carnal Christian: 1 Corinthians 3:1-4

As a young Christian, I was taught that believers are like people with powerful cars. Unfortunately, most of us are not in the driver's seat, but in the back, pushing our cars wherever we go. We need to jump in and turn on the engine. In this analogy, "carnal" Christians are the ones pushing their cars—that is, they rely on the power of their own flesh. "Spiritual" Christians are the ones who have switched on the engine—that is, they have appropriated the power of the Holy Spirit. We can conquer sin if we avail ourselves of the power; it is up to us. This distinction between the "carnal" and "spiritual" Christian comes, I was told, from 1 Corinthians 3:

> And I, brethren, could not speak to you as to spiritual men, but as to men of flesh [or "carnal" men].
> (1 Corinthians 3:1)

Carnal Christians, it is argued, have not yet made the decision to appropriate the power of the Spirit. They are attempting to live out of the power of their flesh; that's why they are called "carnal" or "fleshly." The spiritual Christian, on the other hand, has chosen to appropriate the Spirit's power and so has victory over the flesh. This interpretation of 1 Corinthians 3 understands the logic of the passage in this way:

- Paul is talking to true believers.
- Therefore there must be two kinds of true believers: "carnal" and "spiritual."
- What is a carnal, fleshly Christian? That could only mean one who relies on the power of the "flesh" and so cannot conquer sin. The "spiritual" Christian, therefore, must be one who relies on the power of the Spirit and thus has victory over sin.
- Why aren't all Christians "spiritual"? It could only be because each Christian must decide whether or not to appropriate the power of the Spirit to conquer sin.

Understood in this way, the passage seems to imply the two main beliefs of triumphalism: (1) The power to conquer sin is available in this life (we can overcome the "flesh"); and (2) Christians can freely take this power or leave it (the Corinthians seem to be held responsible for not having become "spiritual").

This perspective is very common in Christian circles today. It has a strong element of truth in that it recognizes the Holy Spirit as the source of spiritual power in the lives of believers. My objection to this teaching begins, however, with the idea that some Christians "appropriate" the power of the Spirit while others do not. As plausible as that might sound, it is far from Paul's intention in 1 Corinthians 3. We can only discover what Paul means by "carnal" and "spiritual" by carefully considering his argument in context.

Is Paul writing to true believers? One of the most common mistakes made in interpreting the New Testament epistles is to assume that the readers of the letters were all genuine believers. We think, "How can their salvation be in question if Paul calls them 'brothers'?" A simple thought experiment shows us how unwarranted this assumption is: Last Sunday, how many pastors throughout the world called their flock "brothers and sisters" while knowing full well that many of the listeners were not believers?

In his letters to the Corinthians, Paul clearly has serious doubts about the salvation of many of them. They may have "believed" Paul when he preached to them earlier, but the values and beliefs that they display in his absence call the true commitments of their hearts into question. Throughout the many issues Paul raises in the Corinthian letters, one theme keeps emerging: There is a group of people in Corinth who reject his authority and who show in many ways their hardhearted disdain for Paul's gospel. For example:

- Paul warns them of the example of the Exodus. Although many Israelites participated with Moses in the miraculous events, they did not share in the blessings of the land because they were idolatrous, immoral grumblers who tested God. The same disastrous fate could await the Corinthians: "Now these things happened to them as an example, and they were written for our instruction, upon whom the ends of the ages have come. Therefore let him who thinks he stands take heed lest he fall." (1 Corinthians 10:11-12)
- Some of the Corinthians have rejected the idea of resurrection from the dead. Paul reminds them of "the gospel which I preached to you, which also you received, in which also you stand, by which also you are saved, if you hold fast the word which I preached to you, unless you believed in vain." (1 Corinthians 15:1-2)
- In exasperation Paul says to his opponents: "Test yourselves to see if you are in the faith; examine yourselves! Or do you not recognize this about yourselves, that Jesus Christ is in you—unless indeed you fail the test?" (2 Corinthians 13:5)

Paul is writing to a mixed group in Corinth. Part of the time he speaks with confidence and praise, thinking of those whose lives show their devotion to the gospel. Other times he uses some of the most stern and sarcastic language in the Bible, thinking of those who challenge his authority and follow the world in its foolishness. By no means does Paul assume that all his readers are truly children of God.

What does it mean to be "spiritual"? In order to understand what Paul means by "spiritual," we must review the situation in the first several chapters of 1 Corinthians. Paul starts his letter to the Corinthians with a strong exhortation:

> Now I exhort you, brethren, by the name of our Lord Jesus Christ, that you all agree, and there be no divisions among you, but you be made complete in the same mind and in the same judgment. For I have been informed concerning you, my brethren, by Chloe's people, that there are quarrels among you. Now I mean this, that each one of you is saying, "I am of Paul," and "I of Apollos," and "I of Cephas," and "I of Christ." (1 Corinthians 1:10-12)

The Corinthians are dividing into cliques and factions, and Paul tells them to stop it. We might easily conclude that Paul's primary concern is unity. He simply wants them to put aside their differences and get back together. Getting along with each other, however, is only of secondary importance to Paul; he has something much more serious in mind. Paul is not as concerned with the *fact* of their disunity as he is with the *cause* of it. Why were the Corinthians choosing sides at all?

Many of the Corinthians think Paul is a sad excuse for an apostle. Compared to the eloquent Apollos, Paul sounds to them like a hayseed, a hick. Accustomed to a sophisticated Greek debating style, the Corinthians are unimpressed with Paul's simple, earnest pleas to believe the gospel. They woefully confuse style with substance. This is always a mistake, but the Corinthians' error is life-threatening. The substance they are ignoring is the gospel itself. Just because Paul doesn't preach in a flashy, worldly style, many are ready to dismiss him. But how can they dismiss Christ's chosen messenger? The Spirit of Christ had revealed to Paul the most important truths in the universe; how can anyone reject him and still claim to be following Jesus?

The Corinthians are starting to look like the seed sown among the thorns in Jesus' parable. Their attraction to worldly wisdom threatens to choke out their initial interest in the gospel. The Corinthians, in fact, are facing a major trial of their faith, and Paul confronts them with the serious choice they face. On the one hand, Paul lacks the flashy, worldly debating style they find so attractive; and yet on the other hand the substance of his teaching is the deep wisdom of the gospel. Which do they really value, style or substance? What is their bottom line?

A believing heart is attracted to the gospel. The story of God's mercy and blessing in Christ makes sense to a believer; it is better than any other story one could hear. When some of the Corinthians reject Paul's ministry because of his style, it calls their faith itself into question. It seems as if any story will do for them, as long as the style is right. Paul is telling them, "Listen to my simple, unspectacular proclamation of the gospel and believe it because it is true; value it because it is the word of life." In turn, if all the Corinthians would agree that Paul's gospel was true wisdom, then they would be united. They would stop dividing into factions because such factions would no longer attract them. They would be united in their love of the gospel and their respect for Paul, the messenger who brought them that gospel.

Now we are in a position to understand what Paul means by "spiritual." What accounts for the fact that some see Paul's gospel as wisdom, while others can't see past his style? It is the work of the Holy Spirit. The "spiritual" person is the one who can see what the rest of the world misses — the gospel as preached by Paul is the true wisdom.

> But a natural man does not accept the things of the
> Spirit of God; for they are foolishness to him, and he
> cannot understand them, because they are spiritually

appraised. But he who is spiritual appraises all things, yet he himself is appraised by no man. (1 Corinthians 2:14-15)

The spiritual person is the one who "appraises" (who understands and rightly assesses the value of) Paul's gospel. What then is the situation of Paul's opponents in Corinth? They understand no such thing; they think Paul is a fool. They are acting like "unspiritual" people; they can't "appraise" Paul's gospel the way a spiritual person should be able to. The presence of factions among them shows the depths of their foolishness.

Paul is not arguing that the spiritual man is free from sin; more accurately, he is arguing that the spiritual man is free from *unbelief*. The sign of spirituality Paul is looking for is not sinlessness; it is, rather, a tenacious belief in the gospel and the wisdom that results. Many of the Corinthians do not fit this description. They have rejected Paul's authority and chosen sides against him, fighting and disputing with each other in the process. Some of them may just be immature; however, Paul is clearly concerned throughout the Corinthian letters that many of them may not be believers at all. In the context of Corinthians, Paul must be saying:

Many of you Corinthians have shown hostility to me and my gospel; the divisions among you are evidence of your worldliness and misplaced values. You act like unspiritual, unbelieving people, whose eyes have not been opened by the Spirit. You must decide whether my gospel is the wisdom of God or not. Ultimately, your choice will show whether the Spirit is at work in you or not.

Am I saying that there is no such thing as a "carnal" Christian? Not exactly. It can be appropriate to say there are two kinds of believers, if we carefully describe what we mean. A person whose faith has been tested and matured is clearly and visibly "spiritual." Paul knows that the Spirit's work in someone's heart leaves a visible mark. Until that mark has shown itself, it is hard to tell the difference between an unbeliever and an immature believer since both act in such a "carnal" way. Thus "spiritual" people are not those who have appropriated the power of the Spirit to conquer sin; they are those who show the work of the Spirit in their mature faith. Yes, their lives have a new moral direction, and their actions show it. But there is no suggestion that they have conquered all their moral failings. Likewise, "carnal" people are not those who have failed to appropriate the power of the Spirit to conquer sin; they are those whose lives have not yet demonstrated any spiritual perception, and thus they may or may not be children of God.

First Corinthians 3 is not contrasting two types of Christians, sinless and victorious Christians versus sinful and defeated ones. First Corinthians 3 is contrasting *mature believers* with *possible unbelievers*. The issue is salvation: Will the Corinthians embrace Paul because they love his gospel, or will their hostility and divisiveness ultimately betray the unspirituality and unbelief in their hearts?

Walk by the Spirit: Galatians 5:16-26
One of the important passages for triumphalism is Galatians 5:

> But I say, walk by the Spirit, and you will not carry out the desires of the flesh. . . . The fruit of the Spirit is love, joy, peace, patience, kindness, goodness, faithfulness, gentleness, self-control.

This sounds like solid evidence for the two principle beliefs of triumphalism: (1) The power to conquer sin is available in this life (the promise "you will not carry out the desires of the flesh"); and (2) Christians can freely take this power or leave it (Christians are commanded to "walk by the Spirit," implying that they might choose not to). Once again, the suggestion is being made that there are two kinds of Christians: those who walk by the Spirit and so have victory over sin, and those who walk according to the flesh and so are defeated by sin. Once again, I believe that this interpretation doesn't fit the argument Paul makes.

First of all, Paul is not counseling defeated Christians on how to obtain a power source. Galatians is a warning to possible unbelievers, to people who are in danger of turning away from the gospel of grace. They have bought the lie that they must please God through their religious obedience to the law. They have been told falsely that only the law promotes godliness; whereas Paul knows that the law condemns us and leaves us with no resources to combat sin. Paul is reminding the Galatians of an important truth: Only when we are freed from the law's demands is there the hope of true godliness. Godliness is produced by the Spirit of God, and as Paul reminds them, "if you are led by the Spirit, you are not under the Law." If the Galatians continue to follow the teachings of Paul's legalistic opponents, they will raise serious doubts whether they are believers at all. Paul does not intend to distinguish between defeated Christians and victorious Christians; he is contrasting legalistic unbelievers with humble believers in whom the Spirit is at work.

Furthermore, it is not at all likely that Paul is talking about sinlessness. A careful examination of the "fruit of the Spirit" shows them to be entirely in keeping with what I would call "Christian maturity" rather than sinlessness. For example, consider the quality of "joy." In many other passages Paul makes clear what he sees as the nature and basis of that joy. For example:

Now may the God of hope fill you with all joy and peace in believing, that you may abound in hope by the power of the Holy Spirit. (Romans 15:13)

. . . Strengthened with all power, according to his glorious might, for the attaining of all steadfastness and patience; joyously giving thanks to the Father, who has qualified us to share in the inheritance of the saints in light. (Colossians 1:11)

You also became imitators of us and of the Lord, having received the word in much tribulation with the joy of the Holy Spirit. (1 Thessalonians 1:6)

In these passages, joy arises from the hope that comes when we firmly believe the gospel. In this life we must persevere through trials and suffering. Why don't we despair? Why don't we just throw in the towel and curse God? Because by the power of the Spirit we believe; our belief gives us hope; our hope causes us to persevere; and this believing, persevering hope, given by the Spirit of God, brings us joy. There is no suggestion in any of this that we are free from sin in the midst of this joy; many mature believers could testify to rejoicing powerfully in hope even while they struggled with their own failures.

The same argument could be made concerning the rest of the fruit of the Spirit. Such spiritual fruit is real and changes the moral direction of our lives, but it does not represent the end of our moral struggle. There is no promise here of sinlessness in this life, but there is a promise of a new spirituality that no unbelieving legalist could ever hope to duplicate.

So then, this "walking by the Spirit" passage provides no support for the triumphalist position. It is not proposing that there are two kinds of Christians—victorious Spirit-walkers and defeated flesh-walkers. Every believer has abandoned the law as a means of pleasing God; every believer "walks by the Spirit" instead. Neither is this passage offering the promise of sinlessness in this life; remember that in Galations 5:5 Paul says, "through the Spirit we are *waiting* for the hope of righteousness." The picture of Christian maturity in Galatians 5 is truly encouraging, but it in no way tells us that we can choose to be completely victorious over sin in this life.

Galatians 5 is contrasting believers with legalists. The issue is salvation. Will the Galatians try to be justified by law-keeping? If so, they will be left with no resources but their own flesh. Or will they turn from the law in belief and walk by the Spirit instead? If they do, then their lives will be marked with the true spirituality that seems to elude them.

Know, Reckon, and Yield: Romans 6:1-14

I don't believe that I have ever read a discussion about sanctification that did not somewhere refer to Romans 6. It seems to provide the most powerful argument for victory over sin that can be found in the Bible. Consider this language:

> How shall we who died to sin still live in it? . . . We should no longer be slaves to sin; for he who has died is freed from sin. . . . Consider yourselves to be dead to sin, but alive to God in Christ Jesus. Therefore do not let sin reign in your mortal body that you should obey its lusts. (Romans 6:2,6-7,11-12)

Many, many teachers, even those who are not total triumphalists, teach that Romans 6 provides the answer to the struggle of sin in the Christian life. The answer is "know, reckon, and yield" — *know* that your old self was crucified with Him; *reckon* yourselves to be dead to sin; *yield* yourselves to God as those alive from the dead. Again, this sounds like solid evidence for the two principle beliefs of triumphalism: (1) The power to conquer sin is available in this life (we are "dead to sin"); and (2) Christians can freely take this power or leave it (Paul implies Christians can choose whether to "know, reckon, and yield"). It's your choice, Christian; the new life is ready to be lived, but you must do the knowing, the reckoning, and the yielding, or else you will remain stuck in your slavery to sin.

In order to understand Romans 6, we must first be clear about the issue Paul is addressing. Paul is not answering the question of how to find victory over sin; he is not providing counsel for defeated Christians. Instead, he is answering the challenge of Jewish legalists, who have charged that Paul's gospel promotes sin. Paul's opponents believe that the *law* is the only way to promote righteousness. If the gospel frees us from our obligation to the law, then we lose all incentive to do what is right.

Paul had finished the previous chapter by saying "where sin increased, grace abounded all the more." That is, God responded to the sins of His people not with condemnation but with an abundance of grace. The legalists can't see the sense of this. Where is the incentive to do good in such a picture? Why not keep sinning so that God can continue to heap on the grace? If our sin makes God look good, why should we try to do what is right? The legalists are charging Paul's gospel with promoting sin. They are not looking for an excuse to sin; they are looking for an excuse to dismiss the cross of Christ. In their eyes, the *law* promotes obedience to God; the cross of Christ only provides an excuse for sinners to keep sinning.

Paul's opponents have greatly misunderstood his theology, and Romans 6 is his response. The interpretive details of this passage are very challenging; we cannot explore them all here. I would say, however, that Paul's answer to them amounts to this:

> If my gospel merely promised a free pass for sinning, then maybe the criticism of these Jewish legalists would make sense. But that is not the gospel at all. In the gospel, forgiveness is only the beginning. Why does God forgive us anyway? So that He can go on to bless us by delivering us from the reign of sin once and for all. We "die with Christ" so that we may walk in newness of life. Does it follow, then, that Christians should yield themselves to sin, as if it were a good thing? No! Knowing that the whole point of the cross was to save them from sin, they should follow their God in the path of righteousness, the righteousness that He has promised for all His people.

Just as in Galatians 5, Paul is not distinguishing between two types of Christians, between those who "know, reckon, and yield" and those who don't. Paul is defending the Christian gospel against the ignorant charges of unbelieving legalists. Does the cross of Christ inspire Christians to pursue sin? No, when we understand the gospel, we see that giving sin full reign in our lives would make no sense. Believers, are you following the true gospel? Then turn from sin and follow God; that is what the message of grace and deliverance calls you to do.

Romans 6 tears down a straw man set up by the legalists— a bogus believer who uses grace to excuse sin. Ultimately, such a person is not possible; the gospel is not an invitation to sin with impunity, but rather a message of salvation from sin. Although believers still struggle mightily with sin, we do in fact struggle. No true believer could embrace sin as a friend.

CONCLUSION

I do not consider my view of the Christian life to be pessimistic. The Spirit of God is working a profound miracle in the life of every believer. We can expect, by the grace of God, to grow in trust, hope, confidence, moral vision, love of God, joy, and in many other ways. Our outward actions will show the reality of this inward revolution. However, I do not believe that the Bible has promised the solution to our moral struggles in this life. Those theological systems that see such a promise have misunderstood the biblical arguments. The question is this: How serious an error is triumphalism? How important is it whether triumphalism is right or I am?

If triumphalism is right, then I have made a serious error. Sin is the source of much suffering and heartache; it certainly has been in my life. I am telling those who struggle with besetting sins that there is no easy answer, that the struggle might go on for some time, and that this is normal. If indeed there *is* an easy answer, then I am seriously misleading myself and any who might listen to me.

However, if I am right, then the error of triumphalism is a serious one. If true victory over sin is not possible in this life, then triumphalism encourages us to deceive ourselves. Do we have victory over sin? Sure, if we squint our eyes just right. If we reduce our concept of sin, if we make righteousness manageable, we can convince ourselves that we have conquered sin. And since victory comes through our own free-will choice, we can congratulate ourselves for having done the right thing. "Hey, I am an overcomer; what's wrong with you?"

Triumphalism can also be a trap for the honest, humble believer. If we recognize we don't yet have victory over sin, then why don't we? Triumphalism always points the finger back at us. God has given us all we need for victory, so if we fail it must be our fault (we don't have enough faith, or we have unconfessed sin, or whatever). We can't ask God for help because God has already done His part. The whole point of triumphalism is that God has already done *everything necessary*; whatever is left to do is ours to accomplish.

At this point we can see how important it is which perspective is right. I am saying that sin is tragic but normal; for a Christian to struggle with sin and fail is a normal part of the Christian life. The struggle itself is strong proof that the Spirit is working in us, for why would we bother to struggle otherwise? Why not just give in? If this is true, then triumphalism can put the struggling believer in a painful and unnecessary bind. What could be worse than being called *abnormal* for something that is *normal*? What could be worse than taking the encouraging fact that we *struggle* against sin and turning it into evidence that we don't know God at all?

Triumphalism is right in many ways. The Christian life has everything to do with holiness, holiness can only come through the Spirit of God, and we can expect the Spirit to do wonderful things in our hearts and lives now, in this life. But triumphalism can be destructively misleading, promoting false hopes, false fears, and false claims for sinless perfection today. Life in the Spirit is not life without sin; it is a life spent learning to hate sin, to love God, and to yearn with an ever increasing passion for the time when God's goodness will reign in our hearts forever.

CHAPTER ELEVEN

What About Free Will?

From my childhood up, my mind had been full of objections against the doctrine of God's sovereignty, in choosing whom He would to eternal life, and rejecting whom He pleased. But I remember the time very well, when I seemed to be convinced, and fully satisfied, as to this sovereignty of God. I have often, since that first conviction, had quite another kind of sense of God's sovereignty than I had then. I have often since had not only a conviction, but a delightful conviction. The doctrine has very often appeared exceeding pleasant, bright, and sweet. Absolute sovereignty is what I love to ascribe to God. But my first conviction was not so.

JONATHAN EDWARDS, *Personal Narrative*

I share Jonathan Edwards' affection for the doctrine of God's sovereignty, but I know that many Christians do not. No topic is more likely to arouse angry, even hostile debates among Christians. Words like "predestination" and "election" are fighting words. So why should I mention this doctrine here? Most Christians can agree on the importance of "faith"; why not just agree to disagree over where faith comes from?

As a person who hates controversy, I would be glad to do so, except for one problem: The doctrine of God's sovereignty is intertwined with most of the major issues of our faith. In my own personal theological journey, I did not set out with any commitment to or even much interest in the sovereignty of God. I wanted to know what the Bible taught about faith and salvation. I found, however, that every step in that journey of understanding confronted me with the issue of God's sovereignty. The gospel is all about a problem with the human will and the solution that God alone can provide. How we conceive of the relationship between our will and God's will affects how we view the gospel itself.

Implicit (and occasionally explicit) in everything I have said in this book is a high view of the sovereignty of God, a view I know to be in the minority among Christians today. I can't assume that my readers agree with me on this important issue. It seems appropriate, therefore, to say something about why I believe this doctrine is so important. And yet the issues are too complex to deal with thoroughly in one chapter. Therefore, I am taking a different approach than I have through the rest of the book. The simplest way I know to deal with this complex topic is to recount my own journey of discovery. At the risk of talking about myself too much, I want to show you how I came to believe what I believe, and why I think it is so essential to understanding the gospel. (This account is simplified and necessarily obscures the very real contribution that many other people have made to my thinking.)

THE BATTLE WITH SIN

I have always identified with Martin Luther—not that I have his courage or wisdom, but I certainly have shared his struggles. Like me, he was driven to understand the Bible out of his knowledge of his own sinfulness. In my own life, moral weakness was obvious and demanded some sort of response. My personal struggles gave me a powerful incentive to understand the Bible, and my initial theological gropings centered around the problem of human sinfulness.

It wasn't long until the question of "free will" came up. As I thought about my own struggles, it was apparent to me that I had to think of "free will" in two different senses. Clearly in one sense I was "free" to do whatever I wanted. Nobody was coercing me; my heart was free to follow its own course. And yet, in another sense, I was not "free." I could decide with my conscious mind that I was going to do right, and yet something deep within me would pull me toward the wrong.

It was a great relief to hear that Paul had experienced the

same struggles: "For the good that I wish, I do not do, but I practice the very evil I do not wish" (Romans 7:19). This is why Paul describes himself as "sold into bondage to sin" (Romans 7:14). Jesus describes that same bondage when He says, "everyone who commits sin is a slave of sin" (John 8:34).

What I found important about passages like these, among other things, was the insight they give into human choices. What we choose is dependent on our "nature." It is not an accident that human choices come out warped and rebellious. To say we are sinners is not just to describe our behavior; it is to describe the inner nature which determines our behavior. We could live a million years and not solve the problem of our own sinfulness because our sinful choices have their source in the inner recesses of the heart.

The same truth, that one's nature determines one's choices, became clear to me when looking at Jesus and His Father. Again, it was no accident that Jesus never sinned. Jesus was purely good; His good choices arose from the goodness of His heart. It would be foolish to say that Jesus wasn't "free." When Satan offered Him the world, Jesus could have accepted—if His heart had taken Him that way. But His heart never would (and never will) take Him that way. The same thing is true of the Father. Who is more "free" than God? And yet God never has and never will do an evil thing; He's not that kind.

I came to believe, therefore, that the gospel itself only made sense in the light of this view of human choices; that is, that our choices are determined by our natures. The gospel includes a promise to restore our hearts from the ravages of sin. Essentially, that amounts to a promise that our free choices are going to stop being evil and start being good. But how can God make such a promise? He can because, unlike us, He has access to our "nature." He *created* us, and He can *recreate* us. I started to see God's reworking of our natures as a recurring theme throughout the whole Bible.

■ Moses told the Israelites that, in future days, God would circumcise their hearts to love the Lord. Where

they had been rebels and enemies of God, they would
instead love, trust, and follow Him. Their choices
would change because God would change their hearts.
(Deuteronomy 30:6)

- Jeremiah told Israel essentially the same thing. God
would write His law in their hearts. The law would
no longer be an external rule that their hearts resisted; it would be an internal reality that changed the
way they responded to God. (Jeremiah 31:31-34)
- Jesus Himself tells us of God's intention to change the
inner man. What else does He mean by being "born
again," if not that our inner selves are reborn, this
time with the inner dispositions of the heart turned
toward God instead of away from Him? (John 3:1-8)
- Paul contrasts our old self with our new self. What is
being made new? Our natures are being made new,
and our choices will follow in newness as well. (See,
for instance, Colossians 3:9-11.)

At this early stage in my thinking, I only had two categories:
(1) Today I am a sinner; and (2) when Jesus comes back my
nature will be changed and I will be righteous. Up to this point
I had thought little about the phenomenon of "faith." What is
the difference between a believer and a nonbeliever now, before
Jesus returns? What accounts for that difference? I was afraid
to consider such questions, for fear I would discover that I did-
n't qualify. The full picture of "faith" as I have described it in
this book would have scared me. To me, the good news was that
God could forgive me and remake my will, both of which I sorely
needed. To talk of what faith ought to look like in this life was
to drag "works" into what was otherwise a comforting picture.

THE LIFE OF FAITH

I did not begin to wrestle with the Bible's picture of what it means
to be a believer until I began to study the book of James. The
seeming tension between Paul and James really bothered me. (I

loved Paul, hated James.) I was totally off-base, of course; chapter eight of this book recounts how I finally reconciled the seeming contradiction. This study in James marked a turning point in my life. For the first time I understood something of what the Bible meant by "belief."

In this book I have used the phrase "righteous sinners" to capture a key distinction in my theology. That distinction started to develop from my study in James, but it caught hold of my theology like a match set to tinder; I saw it everywhere I looked in the Bible. Clearly believers were not yet free from sin, but just as clearly they were highly distinctive from the unbelieving world around them. This "distinctiveness" became the focus of my thinking for many years to come. The book you are reading has been devoted to describing the distinctive nature of saving faith; I won't repeat it here. But once again, I found myself face to face with the issue of God's sovereignty.

I had already seen that sinful choices arise from our natures; I had also seen the promise of the gospel that God would one day in the future solve the problem of sin by recreating our natures. But what about today? What accounted for the profound reorientation of the heart called "faith"? Didn't the choice whether to believe or not also arise from our natures? I began to believe that this must be so. The problem of our *sin* nature would be completely solved one day when Jesus returned; but the problem of our *unbelieving* nature was being solved today.

First of all, I considered the strong emphasis the Bible puts on the testing of our faith. What is being tested? Aren't trials testing our hearts, our natures? If faith is merely an independent choice, grounded in nothing in our natures, then how can it be tested? Today I might freely believe; tomorrow I might freely not believe. What is there to test? A test only makes sense if it is testing something objectively real — the disposition of the heart.

This is exactly the picture I saw in the parable of the sower. The whole point of the parable is to show how the prior condition of the heart determines the response to the gospel. The parable does not deny that real choices must be made; in fact, it insists on it. We must choose whether to believe; we must choose whether to persevere. But it is the prior state of the "soil" which determines the response to the gospel. If our hearts are "honest and good," then we will persevere in faith; if not, then we will show this by our unbelieving response. Our choices show what we are made of, but we did not make ourselves. We do not *choose* what sort of "soil" we are; our choices *reflect* what sort of "soil" we are.

It only made sense, then, to see God as the one who remakes our hearts. The choice whether to persevere in faith is grounded in our natures, our hearts. Why is a believer's nature different from an unbeliever's? Because God has changed it.

At this point I began to reconsider biblical phrases like "circumcision of the heart" and "the new self." I used to think that they referred totally to the future, when sin would be eradicated from our natures forever. But this puzzled me because this interpretation didn't quite fit the language of the passages. I came to believe that such passages were speaking of the profound change at work in the Christian life *now*. To be people who tenaciously cling to their humble trust in God—this is the "new self," the "washing," the "rebirth" of which the Bible speaks. Paul can describe God as the one who "gives perseverance" because perseverance arises from the heart, and God is the Creator and Recreator of our hearts (Romans 15:5).

At this point in my life, the prayers of the Bible started to be very precious and encouraging to me. And what were most of those prayers about? They were prayers that our hearts would be changed, that the way we live our lives would change because God had changed us on the inside. Listen to Paul:

> . . . We have not ceased to pray for you and to ask that you may be filled with the knowledge of His will in all spiritual wisdom and understanding, so that you may walk in a manner worthy of the Lord, to please *Him* in all respects, bearing fruit in every good work and increasing in the knowledge of God; strengthened with all power, according to His glorious might, for the attaining of all steadfastness and patience. (Colossians 1:9-11)

When God fills us with spiritual wisdom, we walk in a manner worthy of the Lord. When we are strengthened with the power of God, we attain to steadfastness and patience in our faith. Why else would Paul seek to change the lives of the Colossians by asking *God* to do it? Our lives change because God acts to change them. This theme emerges most explicitly in this prayer from Hebrews:

> Now [may God] equip you in every good thing to do
> His will, working in us that which is pleasing in His
> sight. (Hebrews 13:20-21)

There is a way to live which is pleasing in God's sight. Is He hanging back, waiting for us to achieve it? No, He Himself works it in us by equipping us in every good thing. Passages like this are consistent with the picture I found emerging from the Bible everywhere: My choices are determined by my nature, and my nature is determined by God.

For me, then, belief in predestination and election were the last step in a long journey. How else could the monumental change of heart which is faith happen unless God makes it happen? Many passages in the Bible seemed to say that God chooses those who will believe and be saved. Given my growing picture of how human choices work, I came to believe that such passages are saying exactly what they sound like they are saying:

- Jesus tells the unbelieving crowds that no one can come to Him and be saved unless the Father draws him, unless the Father grants it to him. Those who don't understand Jesus cannot even hear him because they are children of the Devil. Jesus' sheep, however, hear his voice where others do not. (John 6:44,65; 8:43-45; 10:26-27)
- Paul says that Israel rejected Jesus because their hearts were hardened by God according to His deliberate plan. He tells the Corinthians that the gospel

can only be seen for the wisdom it is by those in
whom the Spirit is at work. (Romans 9-11;
1 Corinthians 2:14-15)

In the light of the picture of faith which I see taught on every
page of the New Testament, passages like these make perfect
sense to me. The Bible tells me—experience tells me—that the
human dilemma starts with the corruption of the will. I believe
in the sovereignty of God because only such a God can reach
and restore the places in my heart where I cannot.

PROBLEMS?

Of course, as I have thought about these issues, I am aware of
the objections that many raise to this doctrine. Why don't those
objections bother me? That question deserves a book of its own,
but I can say a few things.

How Can My Choices Be Meaningful?

Some have argued that, in order to be truly meaningful, our
choice to believe must arise from a place of moral neutrality. If
my choice to believe arises from something in my nature, then
the choice is inevitable and not really "my" choice. How can I
be held responsible for a choice that was not really mine? To
me, it seems just the other way around. How can a choice made
from "moral neutrality" be meaningful, or even possible? If a
choice says nothing about what I am like inside, then it is just
random and meaningless. Of course I can be held responsible for
a choice which arises from my nature; my nature is *me*. If my
heart is bad, bad choices result and I am judged for the evil heart
that led to the evil actions. God is not morally neutral, and His
choices are meaningful. Jesus is not morally neutral, and His
choices are meaningful. Why would I think that I have to be
morally neutral to make meaningful choices?

Still, I know that this objection carries a lot of weight with
some people. They cannot see how their choices can be called
"their" choices if God created the nature out of which they

choose. All I can say is this objection makes no sense to me. If I have the freedom to do exactly what I want, then that is true freedom as far as I am concerned. But the question for me is this: Will I accept the fact that I am not my own creation? My heart expresses itself in my choices, but I did not make my heart. In my own relationship with God, accepting His sovereignty has meant bowing the knee to Him as my Creator, acknowledging that He has the right to do with me as He pleases.

How Can Election Be Fair?

The subject of God's "rights" brings me to another objection: How can it be fair for God to choose some for salvation and not others? This is a huge stumbling block for many, and I understand why. I have felt the force of it myself. But I can think of no better answer than Paul's in Romans 9:

> So then He has mercy on whom He desires, and He hardens whom He desires. You will say to me then, "Why does He still find fault? For who resists His will?" On the contrary, who are you, O man, who answers back to God? The thing molded will not say to the molder, "Why did you make me like this," will it? Or does not the potter have a right over the clay, to make from the same lump one vessel for honorable use, and another for common use? What if God, although willing to demonstrate His wrath and to make His power known, endured with much patience vessels of wrath prepared for destruction? And He did so in order that He might make known the riches of His glory upon vessels of mercy, which He prepared beforehand for glory. . . . (Romans 9:18-23)

The fact that we are God's *creatures* is one of those truths we all have trouble swallowing; here Paul spells out the implications of creation almost brutally. None of us individually has a "right" to God's mercy. He has mercy on some, not because He owes it to them, but in spite of the fact that He does not. God has His good reasons for the choices He makes, reasons based

184 / Crucial Questions

in His purity of character. As our Creator, He has every right to make those choices; that is the answer that Paul gives us, and it is the only answer we will get.

How Can God Be Sovereign and Still Be Good?
If our natures determine our choices, and God determines our natures, then that makes God ultimately responsible for the evil in the world. This blunt statement is one of the biggest reasons many cannot bring themselves to believe in the sovereignty of God. I believe that the Bible presents God as all good and all sovereign; how do we put these two things together? I am tempted to respond, "Who am I to answer such a question?" We are getting into waters over my head. But not to recognize the problem and attempt some sort of answer would be irresponsible.

My basic answer is that the doctrine of sovereignty does not say that God is evil; it says that God in His perfect goodness works through the choices of evil people to accomplish His own purposes. In doing this, He is much like an author who creates an evil character to accomplish the good purposes of the overall book.

Why would God do such a thing? I answer that for myself by asking the question, "What would God's people be missing if the fall of mankind into sin had never happened?" We would never have tasted the bitter fruits of rebellion against God; such rebellion is against life itself, and now we understand that beyond question. We also would never have known God's mercy, which Paul implies in Romans: God made vessels of wrath "in order that He might make known the riches of His glory upon vessels of mercy, which He prepared beforehand for glory" (Romans 9:22-23). Most of all, we would never have known the supreme event in human history. We would never have seen God become a man and die on a cross to save His people.

It might be worthwhile to point out that most who do not believe in God's sovereignty still have to wrestle with the problem of evil. Their usual explanation for evil is that "God allowed evil in order to make free will possible." In other words, even though God knew that much suffering and evil would result from His creation, He did it anyway to accomplish a greater good. Well, I also believe that God uses suffering and evil to accomplish a greater good. No Christian can totally escape the problem of evil. If God exists at all, then He could have intervened in human history to stop much evil and suffering, but for His own good reasons He did not.

God is totally good, and if the doctrine of God's sovereignty implies He is not good, then that doctrine is wrong; I am wrong. But I am convinced this doctrine says nothing evil about God. He created a world that fell into sin because He knew it was the best thing to do. Just as the author of Hebrews says Jesus was perfected through suffering, the same could be said of all creation. Paul says:

> The creation was subjected to futility, not of its own will, but because of Him who subjected it, in hope that the creation itself also will be set free from its slavery to corruption into the freedom of the glory of the children of God. (Romans 8:20-21)

CONCLUSION

So, did we choose God or did He choose us? Both. We chose God with all the freedom creatures can have; God chose us with the fuller freedom that He has as our Creator. This seems both true and essential. God's grace is truly gracious precisely because it can solve the problem we can't solve—the problem of our will. Only He can bring springs in the desert, light in the darkness. The lifetime of choices we must face would be a burden beyond bearing, if God cannot mend our hearts to choose rightly. The sovereignty of God should fill His people with joyful hope. For today, we can hope to find the strength and wisdom to follow Him with a tenacious trust. For tomorrow, we can hope to live a fulfilling life of goodness eternally. This hope is ours because the arm of God is strong to save, strong enough to reach into our souls, recreating us in His own glorious image forever.

Staying on the Narrow Path

—

At one point in *The Pilgrim's Progress,* John Bunyan portrays Christian's path as a narrow road between a ditch on one side and a quagmire on the other. The ditch is that "into which the blind have led the blind in all ages"; I take it to represent the legalism into which the blind Pharisees led their followers (as in Luke 6:39). The quagmire is the one into which "King David once did fall"—that is, the seductive quagmire of licentiousness and sin into which David fell with Bathsheba. Licentiousness on one side, legalism on the other—this is the treacherous path on which Christian must walk. Bunyan tells us:

> The pathway here was exceedingly narrow, and therefore
> good Christian was the more put to it; for when he
> sought in the dark to shun the ditch on the one hand, he
> was ready to tip over into the mire on the other; also
> when he sought to escape the mire, without great care-
> fulness he would be ready to fall into the ditch. Thus he
> went on, and I heard him here sigh bitterly.

Bunyan powerfully pictures the twin dangers each of us must face in our own journey of faith. On the one hand, the true children of God have a new *righteous* orientation; we cannot follow

187

the licentious in their indifference to the moral law of God. On the other hand, the true children of God know themselves as *sinners*; we cannot follow the legalists in pretending to have kept the law successfully. Either of these mistakes is a symptom of a fatal spiritual disease.

Bunyan's story of the narrow path reminds us of Luther's picture of the drunk who, in trying to avoid falling off one side of his horse, falls off on the other side. I love both these analogies; they both say something profound. In a way, however, neither analogy goes quite far enough. One can only fall off a path or a horse on one side, but in fact those who miss the true gospel tend to fall off on both sides at once. In a strange and ironic way, legalism and licentiousness walk hand in hand.

We need to have a clear picture of how deep and deceptive a problem legalism is. Legalism is not just imposing a set of rules like no playing cards, no smoking, and no dancing. Legalism is the deep moral disorder that plagues all mankind. The tendency is to justify ourselves as having kept the rules (whatever those rules might be). Since the heart of legalism is self-justification, of course moral license must accompany it. We must reduce righteousness to a set of doable rules. We cannot let ourselves be judged by the full weight of God's moral law; that is a test we cannot pass. To congratulate ourselves as moral people, we must reduce morality to our size. Thus we can think of ourselves as godly people even as we have neglected the most demanding parts of godliness.

This was Jesus' criticism of the Pharisees. They were legalists, yes, but they were also lawless and licentious. We can see this combination illustrated in Mark 7:

> [Jesus] was also saying to them, "You nicely set aside the commandment of God in order to keep your tradition. For Moses said, 'Honor your father and your mother'; and, 'He who speaks evil of father or mother, let him be put to death'; but you say, 'If a man says to his father or his mother, anything of mine you might have been helped by is Corban (that is to say, given to God),' you

no longer permit him to do anything for his father or his mother; thus invalidating the word of God by your tradition which you have handed down; and you do many things such as that." (Mark 7:9-13)

We admire the movie hero who, caught between the guns of two enemies, ducks and lets them shoot each other. This is essentially what the Pharisees accomplished. They didn't want to think of themselves as ungodly; neither did they want to lose their worldly goods by supporting their parents. Thus their ingenious solution: Dedicate their goods to God so that it would be disobedient to give to their parents. The wealth was dedicated to God in name only; in practice anything declared "Corban" was still available for use. The solution was perfect—they could keep their worldly goods and practice devotion to God at the same time. Never mind that their solution was immoral and disobedient to the larger intent of the law.

Jesus had in mind such sophisticated rationalizations for ungodliness when He warned His disciples, "Beware of the leaven of the Pharisees, which is hypocrisy" (Luke 12:1). In calling the Pharisees "hypocrites," Jesus did not mean they never practiced what they preached; they often did. But when they presented themselves as godly men, they were like actors playing a part. (The Greek word for "hypocrite" refers to actors.) At heart they were not committed to goodness nor sorrowful over their lack of it. The Old Testament religion became a set of rules that they could congratulate themselves for keeping, even as they missed God's purpose for those rules. They pursued a disobedient obedience, an ungodly godliness.

Jesus compared the hypocrisy of the Pharisees with leaven. Such hypocrisy spreads insidiously, corrupting whatever it touches. Jesus' warning is as relevant today as it is was then; hypocrisy did not die with the Pharisees. Religion can be an attractive way to proclaim devotion to God while hiding from Him. Unfortunately, Christianity is as useful a religion for hypocrites as any other. History shows that the leaven of the Pharisees has made its way into the church in every age; it is alive and well today.

In a culture as morally adrift as ours, it is easy for church people to fall into the ditch of legalism. The standard is so low we can easily beat it. We can congratulate ourselves for being conservative and heterosexual and pro-life. Most of all, we have the right religion. We know the right answers about Jesus, the right way to be baptized, the right way to pray. Thank God we are not like other men. At the same time, it is easy to fall into the quagmire of licentiousness. How many of us have baptized worldly ambition and called it "furthering the kingdom of God"? How many churches are split by power struggles on the building committee? How many of us are straining the limits of sexual purity through flirtatious and provocative behavior, all the while congratulating ourselves for "not going all the way"? How many parents are off building great ministries and saving the world while their God-given children are neglected and wandering unguided? All around us are those who name the name of Jesus and look down on their pagan neighbors while at heart they are no different from those neighbors; they watch the same TV shows and pursue the same elicit fantasies and nurse the same grudges and share the same dreams of wealth and success. I say these things not to condemn anyone but as a warning to us all. If we are not pursuing humility and faithfulness before God, then we have lost our way. The leaven of the Pharisees is fatal.

In this book I have tried to answer Joe's questions about faithfulness and failure in his own life. I have argued that he is a "righteous sinner"; he strives after the goodness of God and admits freely when he falls short of it. In the end, only people like Joe will be able to stay on the narrow path, out of the ditch and the quagmire. He cannot be a legalist; to do so would mean denying the reality of his own sin. Neither can he abandon himself to licentiousness; he is learning to love the goodness and moral purity of his Savior. God is good, and Joe is not, but he wants to be. These truths are taking hold of Joe's mind, and through them he has found what he most needs in this world: forgiveness for his weakness and hope for his deliverance. We should all wish to be like Joe.

About the Author

Ron Julian is a teacher at McKenzie Study Center in Eugene, Oregon. During his sixteen years at the Study Center, Ron's focus has been biblical exegesis and communicating the gospel. Ron is also an occasional tutor at Gutenberg College in Eugene, a pastor at Reformation Fellowship, and a frequent guest on a weekly radio program, *In Search of Truth* (which airs from Albany, Oregon).

Ron grew up in California, and he taught in the biblical studies program at Peninsula Bible Church before moving to Oregon in 1981. Ron has a degree in linguistics from the University of Oregon, and has taught Greek and Hebrew, both at PBC and at McKenzie Study Center. In addition to biblical studies, his interests include film, music, literature, and computer technology.

Ron and his wife, Robby, have two children, Brian and Erin.

UNDERSTANDING GOD'S GRACE AND FORGIVENESS

Experiencing God's Forgiveness

This book will help you examine the depth of your sin and guilt in order to appreciate the amazing extent of God's forgiveness in your life.

Experiencing God's Forgiveness
(John Ensor) $12

Transforming Grace

Too many Christians misunderstand grace and try to live up to God's love. But when we understand and accept God's grace, we can live with the freedom of not having to measure up.

Transforming Grace
(Jerry Bridges) $12
Discussion Guide/$7

Get your copies today at your local bookstore, or call (800) 366-7788 and ask for offer **#2036**.